A GUIDE TO
THE MERTON
BLACKWELL
COLLECTION

Compiled and edited by
JULIAN REID, RITA RICKETTS and JULIA WALWORTH

Merton College Oxford
in association with
Blackwell's

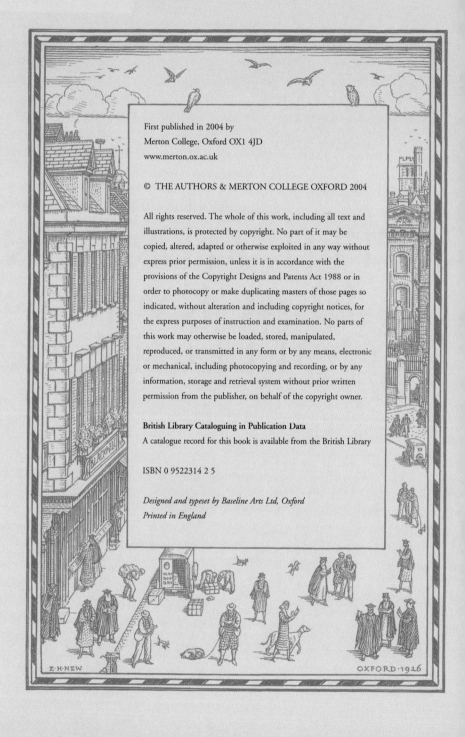

First published in 2004 by
Merton College, Oxford OX1 4JD
www.merton.ox.ac.uk

British Library Cataloguing in Publication Data
A catalogue record for this book is available from the British Library

ISBN 0 9522314 2 5

Designed and typeset by Baseline Arts Ltd, Oxford
Printed in England

CONTENTS

ACKNOWLEDGEMENTS

W<small>E WOULD LIKE TO THANK</small> those who have helped with the Merton Blackwell Collection and the production of this Guide. In particular we are indebted to the Warden of Merton, Professor Jessica Rawson, and Blackwell's President, Julian Blackwell, without whom these projects would not have been realised. Thanks are also due, in equal measure, to many other Mertonians and Blackwellians.

On the Merton side, Michael Stansfield and Sarah Bendall helped to initiate the projects. We would also like to thank the Fellows of Merton College, the College's Development Officer, Jo Osborne (and Jennifer Lewis, her predecessor), members of the Bursary, Jacques Verdon and his staff and the College Porters.

At Blackwell's our thanks are due to the family of Sir Basil Blackwell, especially his daughter Corinna who lovingly preserved a large part of the archives, and to Miles Blackwell (Sir Basil's grandson), Miles's mother Marguerite, and the Executors of his will for adding invaluably to the Collection.

For permission to include and reproduce illustrations, special thanks go to the Directors of Blackwell's Publishing, especially Senior Editor Philip Carpenter, who responded so generously to our many demands. We also express our gratitude to Blackwellians working in Broad Street, especially Manager Philip Bell (and his predecessor John Thwaites), Tony Cooper, Owen Dobbs and Ros Godwin. Others, too, encouraged us in our work: Chairman Philip Blackwell, directors and staff of Beaver House and associated Blackwell companies, particularly Martha Whittaker in the United States.

We are grateful to Judith Curthoys, Robin Darwall-Smith, Martin Maw and Michael Riordan, members of the Oxford Archivists' Consortium, for their guidance and support.

We would like to thank the photographer John Gibbons and the designer Andrew Esson of Baseline Arts.

The Collection has also benefited from the work of Charlotte Swing and Jessie and Jamie Ricketts who have painstakingly transcribed documents.

We also thank our colleagues and family members who have been very patient when we have worked anti-social hours.

Julian Reid, Rita Ricketts, Julia Walworth

*Sir Basil with
the Blackwell
coat of arms in
Merton Hall.*

FOREWORD

Sumite castalios nigris de fontibus haustus (Hilaire Belloc)

THROUGHOUT HIS ADULT LIFE Sir Basil Blackwell maintained a firm bond with Merton College. The connection started in 1906 when Benjamin Henry Blackwell encouraged his son to embark on a university career. Although Benjamin Henry, who founded the famous Broad Street shop in 1879, was completely self-educated, he was determined that his son should have the educational opportunities he had been denied. Showing some of his father's aptitude for Classics, Basil was offered a postmastership (scholarship) at Merton in 1907. As an undergraduate Basil Blackwell's love of classical literature was matched by his enthusiasm for rowing. A series of sporting photographs in the College Archives bears witness to this period in his career. From Merton, Basil Blackwell went on to join the family firm, despite his flirtation with the London publishing scene. Here, as a publisher and bookseller, he served the cause of learning for over sixty years.

In his sixties Basil Blackwell was awarded an Honorary Fellowship at Merton College. His response is said to have been, 'This was my dearest wish: I ask no more'. Merton had been the place of strong undergraduate friendships and intellectual growth. Subsequently, regular attendance at College events and lunches in the Senior Common Room meant that Basil Blackwell was a familiar and loved figure in the College. Many current Fellows recount anecdotes about Sir Basil with evident affection. The College, in turn, benefited from Basil Blackwell's passion for books. Over three decades Blackwell donated to the College Library a series of carefully selected early printed books, the majority produced by the humanist scholar and printer Aldus Manutius, with whom Basil had a particular affinity. These volumes are much valued by the College. In time, Basil Blackwell's name was added to the list of College benefactors, and his armorial shield can be seen in the College Hall. It is appropriate, therefore, that Sir Basil's papers, together with the older records of the family firm, should also come to Merton. Through the Merton Blackwell Collection and the Sir Basil Blackwell Room in Fellows' Quad, the name of Basil Blackwell will continue to be associated with learning and research at Merton.

The Merton Blackwell Collection, as this Guide reveals, charts the course of the success of Blackwell's, the business, from its halting beginnings in 1846 to the end of Sir Basil Blackwell's time in Broad Street. It also reveals Blackwell's inseparability from the people, time and place that made it. Although Basil Blackwell is undoubtedly the central character, the Collection provides glimpses of many other lives, from young boy-apprentices, booksellers and typographers to the grandees of politics, academia, and literature. The Collection shows us generations of readers, writers, poets, academics, and students who frequented Blackwell's.

Within a year of the opening of his 'little shop' in Broad Street, Benjamin Henry launched the imprint, B H Blackwell. Later, his son Basil enlarged the scope of the publishing side. While he kept his father's interest in new poetry alive, Basil also pioneered the publication of school textbooks and was in the forefront of scientific publishing, supporting the broadening of the traditional academic curriculum. Affordable editions of the Classics were produced alongside finely printed collections of belles-lettres. In this way, the university-educated Basil Blackwell was able to fulfil the dreams of his self-educated father and grandfather (Benjamin Harris). When Benjamin Harris arrived in Oxford, he set up a circulating library. A recurrent theme in the Collection, extending over four generations of Blackwells, is a concern for the individual, for education and for the provision of books. Even though the early B.H. Blackwells and their workers were self-made men, they played their own part in the public crusade to secure wider and continuing access to education.

Oxford, too, both as a city and a university, plays an important role in the story: all of the characters in the archive have a connection with Oxford. Blackwell's is an Oxford institution through and through. The first Blackwell bookseller, Benjamin Harris, had chosen to settle in Oxford, opening a small shop just over Magdalen Bridge in 1846, and he was Oxford's first City Librarian. Here, in Oxford, the Blackwells have remained. Today, Blackwell's continues as a meeting place, and reference point, for the Oxford community, town and gown; the Blackwells never could tolerate any divide between the two. But their success was not limited to Oxford. Blackwell's, just as much as the Colleges of the University, helped to forge links with students, teachers and researchers from around the world. The Merton Blackwell Collection provides the reader and researcher with material that helps to explain how a small bookshop, started in a room barely twelve-foot square, became a legend in the academic bookselling world. The Collection forms a rich resource for those studying the history of bookselling, book production and reading in the nineteenth and twentieth centuries, and it provides much material for local and social historians.

Neither the Merton Blackwell Collection nor the Sir Basil Blackwell Room would have been possible without the unstinting enthusiasm and generous financial support of Sir Basil's son Julian. These projects also depended on the work of Sarah Bendall, Michael Stansfield, Julia Walworth, and especially Julian Reid and Rita Ricketts who made Julian Blackwell's designs into a reality. The Blackwells were inspired to support and advance teaching, learning, research and reading for pleasure. In turn, generations of readers and writers drew their inspiration from the Blackwells. The Merton Blackwell Collection will be a permanent memorial to a remarkable family and a great Oxford institution.

Jessica Rawson
Merton College, Oxford, January 2004

Edward Bawden (1903-1989) created a colourful mural showing Oxford and famous Oxford figures throughout the centuries for the Norrington Room in Blackwell's Broad Street shop in 1973. Details from the cartoons (first designs) for Edward Bawden's Oxford *are shown on pages 10, 25 and 54.*

INTRODUCTION

A man should serve the trade by which he lives.

THE BLACKWELLS OF OXFORD have indeed served the trade by which they lived, and for almost two hundred years. But in Sir Basil's view, the book trade was in a league apart. 'As I see it', he wrote, 'there is … a Third estate, unorganised, unvocal, unpredatory, being the commonwealth of those whose commerce is in sharing delight in the noblest products of the spirit of man, in the visual and scenic arts, in music… and, need I add, – in books'. And it was this delight in the sharing of books that made the name of Blackwell's one of the most distinguished in the bookselling and publishing world. But it was the upholding of the tradition of service that brought people to Blackwell's door. In his father's time, Sir Basil recalled, Bishop Stubbs had described Blackwell's shop as having the 'freedom and good fellowship of the tavern, with perhaps the same likelihood of rebuke for wasting time and money on returning home'.[1] When Sir Basil Blackwell was awarded an honorary doctorate, the Public Orator told the members of the Congregation 'that if it were not for the existence of this (Sir Basil Blackwell's) magnificent shop where learned books are sold to every part of the world, you would be scribbling your lucubrations in vain.'

For those who scribbled their 'lucubrations', Blackwell's provided 'free research assistants' and editing services, as well as promoting the sale and publication of any issue. But they also wanted to preserve books, and make them available for future generations. Hearing of a 1659 injunction by Griffin Higgs, sometime Fellow of Merton, demanding that those who had been 'educated in this training ground of youth' should reciprocate, Sir Basil obliged. He was acutely aware of the privilege of a university education, and the first in his family to study beyond elementary school. Among the gifts to his old College were books as varied as Dante's *Le Terze Rime* (Aldine octavo 1502), *Microcosmography* (1732) by John Earle, a seventeenth-century Merton author, and *The Manner of Making Coffee, Tea and Chocolate* (1685), a publication dedicated to a Warden of Merton, Sir Thomas Clayton.[2] Little did Basil dream that his own 'scribblings', together with the archives he had amassed during a long life, would also find their resting place within Merton's portals. But, as the archives reveal so conclusively, the family firm spawned characters as catholic and exotic as any encountered in celebrated published works.

Detail from designs for Edward Bawden's Oxford showing Caveliers and Roundheads. In the windows of the Clarendon Building King Charles I is flanked by an executioner and by his wife, Henrietta Maria.

Chiefly among his varied characters Basil Blackwell revered those, from whatever stations in life, who were bold enough to venture into the 'mind's mountains'. In an early poetry series, Adventurers All, he invites such readers to go with Ulysses on a voyage of exploration: 'Come my friends, tis not too late, to seek a newer world. It may be that the gulfs will wash us down. It may be we shall touch the happy isles. Yet our purpose holds: To sail beyond the sunset'. Athletic 'readers' of the Blackwell archives may indeed sail beyond the sunset, or certainly beyond the grey boxes that house a collection where there is much more than the history of a family firm to be discovered. I hope that this Guide, published to coincide with the 125th Anniversary of the opening of 'Blackwell's of the Broad', entices you to answer Basil Blackwell's call. From among the books, papers, typescripts, documents, catalogues, diaries, love-letters, photographs and paintings we can glimpse a way of life that has all but gone, and stumble on characters whose names are almost forgotten.

Approaching the slopes of the mind's mountains, 'readers', should tighten their safety belts; they will ricochet between Georgian England and the late twentieth century: from the artisan streets of Holborn to a twelve-foot square room in Broad Street, Oxford; from the 'dazzling cloth of buttercup-gold' in Christ Church Meadow to the poppies that linger on the battle fields of the Somme.[3] Vicariously, they can overhear the infighting between publishers and authors, whispers of 'dreadful radical' in the City Council and relive the horrors of the Crimea, which had grabbed early converts to the City Library's Reading Room. They can be called to the underworld of the Bodleian and surface to hear the plash of oars on the Cherwell. Lifting their eyes to Matthew Arnold's Cumnor, they can sympathise with the temptations facing Victorian trades people, eavesdrop on the goings-on in the local magistrates courts and come to rest by the honesty-spangled grave of the first B.H. Blackwell (Benjamin Harris), in St Cross cemetery. It is here with Benjamin Harris that the Blackwell story begins, or, looked at in another way, very nearly floundered.

Benjamin Harris Blackwell, with his brother, Isaac, and wife-to-be, Nancy, arrived in Oxford in the early 1830s.[4] He had migrated from London's East End, where his father was a tailor. Eschewing his father's trade, although 'his intended' was a skilled embroideress and dressmaker, Benjamin Harris started a 'circulating library of standard works'. From 1831 until his death, he was also the librarian of the local Temperance Society, which he founded with his brother on their arrival in Oxford.[5] A passage from the *British and Foreign Temperance Intelligencer* records Benjamin

Harris's teetotal activities: '... We are bold to demand a standing for the improvement of man, physically, socially, morally and intellectually; we have taken two spacious rooms in the centre of the city, one for reading and one for refreshment, which we have thrown open to the public at a moderate charge; furnished with temperance and other periodicals, and an increasing lending library of standard works....'[6]

Putting up a stand for the improvement of man must, however, have provided Benjamin Harris with a modest income. A receipt exists, dated 2 January 1846 (due 21 December 1845), showing a payment of 'four pounds and ten shillings being one quarter rent of a House (in fact, a small ground floor property) in St Clements'. The local trade directory of 1846 confirms that Benjamin Harris, then aged thirty-three, had put the name B H Blackwell, Bookseller, above the door of 46 High Street, St Clements. It was sandwiched between the trading establishments of William Loder, Pork Butcher, and Samuel Prince, Baker, and next-door-but-one to J B Cardi, Professor of French. Family stories reflect a maverick pride in this audacious choice of site. Benjamin Harris had opened the shop as near as possible to the City's boundary, refusing on principle to submit to the tyranny that only a freeman of the City, or the son or apprentice of a freeman, 'might set up a new business in Oxford without the payment of a fine'. From this site in St Clements the first B.H. Blackwell combined the roles of bookseller, teetotal librarian, and father of three children. And as if he did not have work enough, he also set out to 'improve the standing of man' in a wider context, holding down the post of Librarian of Oxford City's first Public Library.[7]

The post of Librarian was no sinecure, and Benjamin Harris worked long into the night and at weekends. But he still found the energy to expand his bookselling business, preparing catalogues to inform potential overseas customers about his stock. A bill survives, dated 11 January 1853, for the production, by the Oxford Chronicle, of 250 catalogues of twelve pages. Somehow these catalogues must have found their way across the ocean since there is a record of a parcel of books, invoiced for £4.14s, being received by a Mr John Gooch of Pennsylvania on 17 March 1853. He replied to 'Mr B.H. Blackwell' on 30 May 1853, settling the account and wishing to be remembered to Mr Richards, a 'rival' bookseller and close friend of the Blackwell family. Mr Gooch also intends further contact: 'If you find it worthwhile I shall be glad to see your catalogue as you carry it on...much wishing you increase of profitable business'.

At home, now in more comfortable quarters in Turl Street, Benjamin Harris concealed his ill health. The shocking tale of Benjamin Harris's untimely death was later recorded by his granddaughter, Dorothy. 'One Sunday after lunch', she wrote, 'B.H. Blackwell the First died suddenly in his chair'. But, she added, he left behind 'a little, rather grave, boy of seven', who was 'to grow up in a home struggling with poverty and a life in which there was no time, or room, for fun.'[8] This 'little boy' was her father, Benjamin Henry, who was destined to revive the name of B.H. Blackwell, bookseller. And here in Oxford the firm of Blackwell's has remained, serving the trades of bookselling and publishing into the fifth generation.

Merton's generosity in providing a home for the Blackwell archive ensures that their stories will not be lost. The Collection charts the adventures of the first three generations of B.H. Blackwells: Benjamin Harris, Benjamin Henry and Basil Henry, and sheds light on the work of the next two: Richard and Julian Blackwell, and their sons: Miles, Nigel and Philip, who all became Blackwell Chairmen. But for over a decade after the death of Sir Basil Blackwell in 1984 the various documents and effects making up the archive had lain unread. There was a pressing need to find them a permanent, more durable, home lest, as Goethe cautioned: 'We lay aside never to read them again, and at last we destroy them out of discretion'. When Julian Blackwell retired as Chairman he handed me the task. To the existing archives, I was able to add letters, manuscripts, paintings and miscellaneous objects left to Julian by his father, material generously bequeathed by Miles Blackwell, documents lovingly preserved by Sir Basil's daughter Corinna and other Blackwellians. But where to put them? The papers themselves, with which I had become familiar during the writing of *Adventurers All*, pronounced their own palpable decision: Merton! Curious, people asked me 'why Merton'? The answer was simple. Sir Basil Blackwell loved the College, and members of the College loved him[9].

There was another reason for ensuring that the papers reached Basil Blackwell's old College. His father, Benjamin Henry, who founded the famous Broad Street shop and the publishing house, had never himself received a university education. He was forever a scholar manqué, albeit rather a good one. Plans to award him an honorary degree failed to materialise in his lifetime, but his shop came to be regarded as one of the 'better Colleges of the University'. Benjamin Henry's joy when his son was awarded a scholarship at Merton can only be surmised; he was too modest to write of it. As a teacher with experience in higher, further and secondary education, I have seen at first-hand the look on the faces of parents, particularly if they had not themselves had the privilege, when their offspring gained places at university or received their degrees. I could so easily imagine the gratitude Benjamin Henry, and his teacher-wife Lilla, must have felt towards Merton. And serendipitously, I found a note, in Benjamin Henry's handwriting, suggesting that his brother Fred had been a chorister at Merton. So it was that I had the temerity to telephone the then Librarian of Merton, Sarah Bendall.

Won over by the merit of the archive, which needed no other advocate, Sarah Bendall sought the all-important approval of the Warden. Happily, Professor Jessica Rawson consented, as did Julia Walworth, the current Librarian. Julian Blackwell added his whole-hearted support. The subsequent removal of the bulk of the archive to a temporary home in the College was not without its lighter moments as the Librarian, Archivist and I played amateur removals. The College porters stood by enigmatically, making a mental note to recruit us in future, while we solicited further help from any Fellow who, passing by, was rash enough to make eye contact. Although the main archive will be permanently housed in Merton College Library, some items will be on display in the Broad Street shop. So while the archive is now in safe and fitting hands, and the contents expertly ordered and documented in this Guide, I cannot resist one last chance to describe some of my favourite themes, encounters, and 'friends' made among the Blackwell papers, and to draw attention to stories that may not before have had a public airing.

All three B.H. Blackwells advanced the cause of universal education, at every level, and the last two did much to improve local conditions in the workplace, for all they were sticklers too. Of the three, it was Basil who had the most leisure and means, when he inherited a family business in fine fettle, to extend the range of public or community service. His commitment to the reform of the justice system was well known, as was his humanity as a long-serving Justice of the Peace. At the same time, like his father, he played a leading role within the bookselling and publishing fraternity, traditions carried on by his sons and grandsons. But given Basil's abject refusal to court the right people in the right place, his Knighthood, the first to the book trade, was even more remarkable. He did after all come from a line of individualists, mavericks even. Great-grandfather Joshua had cocked a snook at the government of his day, refusing to drink as a means of reducing excise returns. Benjamin Harris agitated for the introduction of licensing laws, with deputations to 'Lord Peel's Licensing Commission', and he publicly berated the medical profession for failing in its duties to alert citizens to the dire effects of alcohol. In their stead he arranged public lectures, charging an entry fee of 2 pence, where experiments were conducted to demonstrate the dubious nutritional value of 'malt liquors'. The pamphlets advertising the meeting do not go into the details, but the mind boggles!

Benjamin Henry, like his father, was in no man's pocket, and his wife Lilla ensured that he stayed that way. His sister Matilda went as a missionary to South Africa, while his brother-in-law Jack went as a fur trapper to Canada. Basil Blackwell fought battles that he could have ignored in his comfortable life: the 'Ring', the Post Office, saving the hand-printing presses, rescuing the public from the depravity of *Last Exit to Brooklyn* and *Lady Chatterley* and regime change in Oxford's traffic management. His sister Dorothy was a doughty character, fearlessly stalking the corridors of a London hospital as a matron throughout the Blitz. Basil's children also displayed unconventional traits, and he termed the tribe (five) of them 'philistines'. Yet they were anything but; their father surrounded them with the writings of the Greeks and remnants of the Arts and Craft Movement, and they cut their philosophical and political teeth on the tenets of guild socialism. Their father, they soon saw, for all that he was a successful businessman, always remained an idealist. He clung to the idea that the individual had the power to 'do good', a creed he tried to practice as well as preach. Haunted by the memory of the deaths of so many friends in the savagery of the First World War, he thought of contacting 'the Pope or some other Christian leader' to see if 'spiritual appeasement' could avert the course of the Second. But 'unfortunately', Basil wrote 'before I could put this idea to the Vatican or to Canterbury, Germany had invaded Poland'.[10]

Basil's belief in the individual was not limited to the world stage. It characterised his dealings with staff in his shop. In this he was his father's son. Both men, as respective chairmen of the family business, sought to extract a liberal synthesis from the competing political ideologies of capitalism and socialism which would enable them to run a business where the individual benefited from both systems. Employees were 'members' of the family and trained as 'craftsmen' not 'workers', and rewarded with above-average wages. Running against the establishment, the Blackwells agitated for a shorter working week and encouraged and paid for their employees to 'better' themselves, enabling them to go to evening classes and, later, to study for extra-mural degrees. Before there was any statutory regulation, the Blackwells had devised schemes that gave their staff share holdings, annual paid holidays and pensions. Above all, staff had 'ownership' in the business and the chance to go from the bottom to the top rung of the ladder; in Sir Basil's day they even convalesced in his own home at Appleton. And the Blackwell's shop itself was designed to attract a broad church; it was not just the province of the academic elite, but for families, children and those seeking to educate themselves.

The approach that Basil and his father took to publishing combined idealism and respect for scholarship in the widest sense, rather than hard-nosed commercialism. Volumes of poetry, including the series Adventurers All, were often published at the Blackwells' own expense, but so also were works by well-known writers, among them the Sitwells and William Morris.

The close relationship between Basil and his 'writers', in the days when a publisher could personally oversee his lists, may mistakenly leave the impression that he was chiefly a midwife, delivering the literary offspring of others. Yet, as the archives reveal, Basil was a prodigious and scholarly writer in his own right. Although he never produced the full-length book he dreamed of, his scholarship was nonetheless recognised. In 1964 he served a term as President of the Classical Association and in 1970 as President of the English Association. At the inaugural ceremony, he regaled his colleagues with a lecture modestly entitled 'The Origins of the Classics'.[11] His grandfather and father, too, had dabbled in writing. While Benjamin Harris's literary epistles were aimed at converting alcoholics and reminding the authorities of their responsibilities, his son went on to dabble in poetry, wrote long commentaries for Oxford's tourist guides and was also something of a diarist. These diaries, together with his letters, a few of his mother's and a number from Lilla before and after they were married, have become special favourites.

In his fine spidery hand, almost every word requiring a magnifying glass to transcribe, Benjamin Henry recorded his daily life as an apprentice, and then manager, the books he read, his accounts, his regular choral singing, his 'indulgence' as a member of the local rowing club, morning runs around Christ Church Meadow, where he rehearsed chunks of Milton, and musical suppers, after Sunday Evensong, in his mother's rooms in Holywell Street (where he paid her 12/6 in rent). The diaries also tell poignantly of his attempts to rule out temptations in the wilds of Oxfordshire and of his breast-beating repentances. From his letters we know that Benjamin Henry was already pledged to a farmer's daughter, Lydia (Lilla) Taylor, from Blo Norton, in Norfolk. But neither of the parties were free to marry, both feeling responsible for their widowed mothers. It is clear from his letters to Lilla that Benjamin Henry was passionate about her, and he kept her informed of any improvements in his material situation, such as pay rises. But being a long way off, with limited opportunities to meet his intended, Benjamin Henry took solace in friendship. His favourite woman friend was Nellie Ogden, who he thought 'brilliant' and full of 'vivacity'. Wistfully he notes 'how domesticated she was and what a good wife she would make, if she could only love. But Nellie seems too sensible to lose herself in such a passion'.[12]

It was Nellie Ogden who had introduced the twenty-six-year-old Benjamin Henry to her old friend Mary (Polly) Barwell, on one of their many water excursions. Polly, the nineteen-year-old daughter of a successful seed merchant from outside Oxford, was 'very aimiable, of a cheerful and yielding disposition but indifferently educated and with a slight knowledge of the world'. Benjamin Henry confided to his diary: 'I could not fail to see that I had made an impression on her. Though I was extremely careful not to let her see that I knew it. I was charmed by her face and manner and felt flattered by her notice'. And, despite his conscience, he could not resist a little dalliance. He rashly sent 'two photographs with a little off-hand note saying 2/3 High Street was a bad place to write letters', thus hinting that her answer (which he 'expected, and thought might be rather gushing') had better come there. On the third day it came, beginning '*Dearist* Mr Blackwell' and 'continued in a similar strain'. Feeling guilty, Benjamin Henry replied with 'a plain letter detailing the history of his former engagement under the name of 'Mr A'. Despite his attempts to disengage, one or two letters followed, 'getting warmer and warmer on both sides', and there were other meetings when a few kisses were snatched, even though the couple were chaperoned by Nellie. But Benjamin Henry was out of his depth.

Pouring out his anquish in his diary, Benjamin Henry laments that 'my happyness, my honour, uprightness, everything seemed to vanish in a moment beside a feeling of my foolishness together with a sense of displeasure of God who seemed to hide his face from me leaving me a prey to bitter regrets'. Eventually, Benjamin Henry summoned up the courage to write a parting letter. Just before Advent, he writes, 'I received a parcel sent c/o Mrs Ogden containing a few books given by me to her (Polly) and a very curt letter from her brother (who had encouraged her in her correspondence with me) saying that every scrap sent by me had been destroyed' and that Polly 'regretted her folly sincerely'.[13] Meanwhile, Benjamin Henry's mother Nancy knew nothing of this.

Benjamin Henry's diaries reveal the great debt he felt he owed his mother, and his need to present a good account of himself: theirs was not a modern confessional relationship. But, as their correspondence shows, it was nonetheless warm and very loving; Nancy was clearly very partial to Lilla and, perhaps atypically, rejoiced in the idea of sharing a house with the couple when they should be married.[14] Benjamin Henry never forgot that his mother had ensured the family's survival, resuming her trade as a needlewoman after the death of his father. The Oxford directories confirm Nancy's occupation as 'dressmaker', and successive yearly entries reflect the family's setbacks and recoveries. Forced to move from 'The Turl' after her husband's death, she went to the back streets of Jericho, on to 'Jews Walk' and then to more commodious rooms in Holywell, where she had a maid and a pupil in residence. She never owned her own house, and ended her days living with her son 'over the shop'.

Benjamin Henry's diaries also tell of his rigorous programme of reading and sitting up playing cards until the small hours ('winning £1/1? at speculation' though he 'gambled rashly'). But somehow he also managed to build up his business contacts and expertise, undertaking what he described as 'private work': 'some free and some charged'.[15] By March 1876 he had amassed a small collection of books valued at £26/16/0, 'to bear a profit, if sold, of 15-20%'. Benjamin Henry, whose interests included map making, travelled widely through the English counties to make his purchases, aided by the spread of the railways: London to Pontefract, Hampshire to Herefordshire, Sussex to Surrey and Southsea, Leeds to Cardiff, Durham to Suffolk, Edinburgh to Lincoln. Interestingly, he bought a considerable number of books from clergymen and schoolteachers; these were the 'poorer professionals' who, often finding themselves in straitened circumstances, were glad of the services of a sort of 'intellectuals' pawnbroker'.

Benjamin Henry's list of purchases reveals his eclectic taste and wide interests: from books on steam engines, which he later studied and modelled, to natural history, angling, Ruskin's strict guidelines to would-be painters and (Andersen's) fairy tales. But more predictably there were works of poetry and the Classics from Horace to Milton and Wordsworth, and essayists and diarists such as Lamb and Boswell. Disraeli, in seven volumes, led the vanguard in social and political comment and Mountstuart Elphinstone's *History of India* (1841) may have anticipated Benjamin Henry's subsequent dabbling in the new markets of the Empire. Continuing his own efforts at 'self-education', Benjamin Henry assembled a collection of Latin dictionaries, primers, Arnold's *Latin Prose* (part 1 with key, 1871) and Brooke's

Benjamin Henry
Blackwell :
in business 'on
his own account'

Primer of English Literature (1876). There were works of translation from many eras, including an edition of King Alfred's Anglo-Saxon Orosius. Gifts, too, featured in the list: a gift from the Bishop of Gloucester and Bristol of an 1860 English Bible, for example. But education for Benjamin Henry was a long-term project, and a 'lack of it', in the formal sense, was not to deter him, despite his failure to get the post of City Librarian in Cardiff. In the preamble to his 1877 diary he wrote of his resolve to 'keep a check upon my spending and save if possible 100 pounds in the course of the next two years'.

By January 1877 Benjamin Henry had been with Mr Rose (bookseller) as an assistant manager six years and seemed 'likely to stay at least for another two', but at the end of that period he hoped 'to be able with a little assistance to open in London or elsewhere a business on my own account'. He had £30 in his PO Savings Bank and books to the value of £40 (an increase of £14.00 in one year) calculated to bear a profit of 15% to 20%. By the autumn of 1878 he was on his way to reviving his father's name: on 1 January 1879 the name B H Blackwell, Bookseller, went up over a door in Broad Street. Within two years he brought his mother to live 'over the shop', which prospered at such a rate that he was able to contemplate marriage to Lilla, in 1886. Two children, Dorothy and Basil, followed at a pace, and Lilla passed on to them her own stories, as well as those of the old Blackwells, which they subsequently recorded. Lilla's stories, which she heard from her husband and mother-in-law Nancy, give the archive a very different perspective; not only do they reveal her lively character but they give additional insight into the next generation of Blackwells, particularly Basil. Lilla's exuberance and zest for life provided a counterbalance to Basil's more sober father, and she passed on something of her 'country air about her', which perhaps explains how easily Basil later fitted into village life in Appleton.[16]

Lilla, together with her four sisters and one brother, Jack, enjoyed a carefree and happy early childhood. From Dorothy, we learn that the family lived in a roomy and pleasant farmhouse, 'with French windows opening onto the lawn, and hanging creepers'. Her father, owning and farming his own land in the Norfolk village of Blo Norton, 'was much respected as an honest and upright man', but he could do nothing to stem the downturn in the price of corn. The livelihood of small farmers in rural England was being threatened by the reform of the Corn Laws. Unable to contend with the influx of cheap corn from Canada, John Taylor's farm was one of the hundreds that went under the hammer.

Lilla often told of the day the farm was lost. Watching her father from an open bedroom window as he stood in the courtyard below, she saw the whole disastrous spectacle of 'his horses and possessions all being sold'. John (Jack) Taylor died before his wife, a broken-hearted man, and Lilla always felt deeply for her father, whose 'good strong life was largely unrewarded'.[17] This family tragedy kept Lilla at home until she was in her thirties; working as a teacher enabled her to save the family house. She was only able to escape to Oxford after her mother's death from cancer.

Lilla's stories enliven the Collection and remind the reader that the Blackwell women were every bit as impressive as their menfolk. Dorothy, a matron who tended casualties during the London Blitz, was as fearless as her forbears; she, too, was cast in the mould of her mother Lilla and her grandmother Nancy. Just as Lilla's stories had informed the third generation of Blackwells (Dorothy and Basil), so Dorothy wised up her brother's five children, three of whom were female, and had personalities as strong as their brothers'. More is gleaned about the fourth generation of Blackwells from the letters of Basil's wife, Marion Christine (Soans) Blackwell (1888-1977). Christine's own life, however, remained very private, and few knew that she was a Classics scholar with a First from London University, working before her marriage for the Greek scholar Gilbert Murray, an avid, and eloquent, champion of women's rights. After marriage, when her husband was kept at work even in the holidays, she took the children to her parents' house in Ramsgate. But she wrote to Basil that her father disapproved of her short hair, and of her inability to manage her ill-mannered children.

Christine Blackwell's letters give an insight into the joys of seaside holidays for a parent alone, and, in this, time has changed nothing. Richard Blackwell, her eldest son, was prone to throwing things at the dinner table, while her eldest daughter, 'simply above herself' insisted on sharing her mother's bed. But Basil was not let off the hook; Christine's letters contained teasing invitations 'not to forget me', as she pleaded with Basil, 'When will you ever arrive?' For her, holidays proper only started when Basil was safely ensconced on the beach, complete with bucket and spade. Later with five children now in tow, Christine and Basil opted for independence. Renting a house in Anglesey or Cornwall, the Blackwell gang would declare war, 'Swallows and Amazons' style, on any 'friends' in the vicinity. On winter evenings board games and books were the standby, broken only by Christmas festivities when Christine would organise a rigorous programme of 'family performances'. Set in the sitting room, with the library curtains pulled across, the Blackwell Thespians resurrected the hero king 'Croton Hoton Thologos', and mounted other home-spun productions.[18]   Under Christine's direction no one, however retiring, was spared.   Sir Adrian Mott recalled the 'intense agony' of being forced to dress up, and 'once she even went so far as to insist on my playing the flute (fortunately behind the scenes), to everyone's alarm and despondency'.

Other characters and details also emerge from the archive, ones that provide a vivid picture of country life between the Wars. Just as Fred Hanks, Blackwell's first apprentice-director, had guarded Benjamin Henry's two small children, so Cuthbert White, a member of the famous Appleton White family, was surrogate parent to Basil's youngest son Julian. It was from Cuthbert that both Julian and his mother learned the lore of the countryside and the mores of village (Appleton) life. Julian was trained by Cuthbert to chop the firewood, but even his delight at being allowed to 'play' with a sharp axe was eclipsed by Cuthbert's invitation 'to help him tinker with the family motor'. Julian was instructed to perch on the front of the bumper, facing away from any on-coming traffic, and cling onto the headlights, listening out for the 'wrong clinks' as Cuthbert drove the offending machine rather too fast. Christine Blackwell was not a nervous mother, and she was too busy to notice the minutiae of her youngest offspring's 'adventures'. For his part, Julian revelled in his relative physical freedom. Spending long afternoons on the river in his own small boat, he was free to 'be a bit frightened', to avoid his censorious siblings and to sort out his childhood fears and dreams. Julian would return to a warm kitchen, a fresh-baked cake; his mother would fend off her husband who was apt to be a hard taskmaster.

Throughout their long life together, Christine and Basil were bound together by a fierce loyalty; Basil likened their partnership to that of Matthew Arnold's 'bright and aged snakes', and Christine called it 'injury time'.[19] And so the stories and myths continue to unfold as the Merton Blackwell Collection is catalogued. The archive brings back to life many who would otherwise moulder in George Eliot's unnamed tombs, while resonating with the same social, political and economic forces that shape our present lives. Writing in 1976, Richard Blackwell asked that any history of the firm should reflect this matrix.[20] But in researching the archive, and writing up material, I have handled 'the goods': drafts, diaries and love letters. And I now feel rather like Basil Blackwell's grocer who 'cracks a bottle of fish sauce, or stands himself a cheese'. I have made 'friends' among the Blackwell papers, and I am loathe to part from them. But common sense and probity, a favourite virtue in Benjamin Henry's book, forced me to entrust them to the safekeeping of the experts at Merton, Julia Walworth and Julian Reid, who came to stand side by side with the admirable Blackwells in my affections. They are now the starting place for Sir Basil's 'athletic readers'. Those who adventure in the Merton Blackwell Collection will have to forgo the 'paste-pot and the pair of scissors' much relied on by Benjamin Henry and Basil Blackwell, but they will be well advised to cultivate their 'horse-sense'.

Basil Blackwell, who never took himself too seriously!

Detail from designs for Edward Bawden's Oxford *showing King Henry VIII and Cardinal Wolsey in the foreground. To the left, Thomas Linacre flies a kite for the College of Physicians.*

A GUIDE TO THE MERTON BLACKWELL COLLECTION

THE MAJORITY OF THE RECORDS that make up the Merton Blackwell Collection were transferred to the College in the summer of 2002. The archive consisted mainly of documents, photographs, and some paintings, which had been stored above the old Blackwell's Children's Bookshop. Other material in Sir Basil Blackwell's Office in the Broad Street shop still remained to be rediscovered. Happily, other material, too, came to light: records and effects that had been left by Sir Basil to his son Julian and grandson Miles. Through their generosity these bequests have now greatly enriched the Collection.

The Blackwell Collection contains both business and personal papers. The business archive consists of the historical records of B H Blackwell's (now Blackwell's) and of its associated publishing companies, principally Basil Blackwell Publishing and the Shakespeare Head Press, with examples of the published works of B.H. Blackwell, Basil Blackwell and Mott, the Shakespeare Head Press and Blackwell Publishing. The personal papers cast light not only on the firm, but on the life and times of many other associated Blackwellians. Letters, diaries and the published and unpublished writings of outsiders and insiders illuminate the lives of Blackwells, the family firm and the wider world of books. In particular, the writings of Sir Basil himself are a major resource. The Collection joins the noteworthy early printed books given by Sir Basil to the College Library during his lifetime.

Although the body of the Collection is housed in Merton College, some material will remain on display in the Gaffer's Room in Blackwell's Broad Street shop. This present Guide serves to introduce the Merton Blackwell Collection. It is a work in progress. The detailed cataloguing of the Blackwell Collection will continue, and will be extended to include newly discovered material. The final detailed catalogue will eventually be made available online at the Merton College web site.

The Guide has been organised to reflect the range of the firm's work, the wider Blackwell family and those associated with them. The earliest entries refer to the bookshop opened by the first B.H. Blackwell, in St Clements in 1846. The main listings, however, continue with the business papers of Benjamin Henry Blackwell, who founded the world famous shop in Broad Street in 1879. These papers were housed in his workroom, as were those of his successor, Basil Henry Blackwell. (Although Sir Basil became chairman in 1924, on the death of his father, he was always known as the 'Gaffer' and his 'workroom' became the Gaffer's Office; it was the equivalent of a managing director's office in a larger company.) Added to these are the records of the subsequent chairmen: Richard and then Miles Blackwell.

Next come the records of the principal Blackwell firms—the bookshop and publishing company—then the subsidiaries and dependent bookshops. Personal papers of members of the Blackwell family appear in the later part of the Guide. Where there are significant series of records for individual companies, for ease of reference these have been listed in the order Corporate, Financial, Customer, Staff, Property, Marketing and Miscellaneous. Additional subdivisions have been made in the case of Basil Blackwell, reflecting the breadth of his activities, and of B H Blackwell's bookshop, to accommodate different departments and premises.

How to obtain access to the Collection

Merton College Library welcomes bona fide readers engaged in research, whether for personal or academic reasons. The Blackwell Collection is available by appointment. Readers are asked to register upon arrival, provide proof of identity and to observe certain regulations regarding the handling and care of the Collection. Requests for access to the Blackwell Collection at Merton College can be made in writing or by email either to the Archivist or the Librarian, Merton College, Oxford OX1 4JD.
Email: archivist@admin.merton.ox.ac.uk

Julian Reid
Merton College

Blackwell's Business Records

Benjamin Henry Blackwell, founder of B H Blackwell's, Broad Street, 1879

Benjamin Harris Blackwell

Born in London, he settled in Oxford in the 1830s, where he opened a second-hand bookshop and circulating library in St Clements. Also librarian of the Oxford Temperance Insititute and first public librarian of the City of Oxford, he died from overwork in 1855.

Invoice of *Oxford Chronicle and Berks. and Bucks. Gazette* with Mr. Blackwell of 3 Turl Street, for printing 250 catalogues, 9 February 1853; copy of letter from George Routledge to Nancy Blackwell cancelling outstanding debt for books ordered before the death of her husband, Benjamin Harris Blackwell, 20 June 1855.

Benjamin Henry Blackwell (Mr Blackwell)

Opened B H Blackwell's bookshop at 50 Broad Street, Oxford, 1 January 1879. Founding member of the Oxford and District Branch of the Booksellers' Association, 1899, and President of the Antiquarian Booksellers' Association, 1913. Founding Chairman of B H Blackwell Ltd., 1920, until his death in 1924. Relatively little material survives from this period; it is believed that many records were lost during the extension of Blackwell's premises in Broad Street in 1937. Surviving records appear to have been preserved principally on account of their content or authorship.

Correspondence, incl. letters from W. Wade Fowler, Robert Bridges, H.C. Beeching and Hillaire Belloc, c.1881-1924.

The Horace Club

The Horace Club was founded by Arnold Ward in March 1898 and existed until 1901. As well as Ward its members included Raymond Asquith, Hilaire Belloc, John Buchan and St John Lucas, among others. According to the printed rules of the Club each member was to produce a poem 'in a well-known language...not exceeding in length, nor falling below in brevity, any poem of Horace (excluding De Arte Poetica)'. These autograph poems were pasted into two albums – the 'Records' – kept by Benjamin Henry Blackwell, which he subsequently published as *The Book of the Horace Club*.

Horace Club 'Records', 1898-1901; printed material relating to the Horace Club, including notices of meetings and copies of membership rules, 1898-1901.

Basil Blackwell (The Gaffer)

Basil Blackwell joined B H Blackwell's in 1913 to run the publishing department, after a year at the London office of the Oxford University Press. He founded the separate publishing company of Basil Blackwell and Mott Ltd. with his old college friend Adrian Mott in 1922 at 49 Broad Street. Upon the death of his father, Benjamin Blackwell, in 1924, Basil Blackwell also assumed the

'The Gaffer in his Broad Street office', c.1935

Chairmanship of B H Blackwell Ltd., running both companies form the small office on the first floor of 50 Broad Street which came, in time, to be known as the Gaffer's Room.

Correspondence

The business correspondence of Basil Blackwell is one of the larger series of primary material in the collection, excluding series of printed material, such as sales catalogues and the staff newsletter, *Broad Sheet.* The correspondence generated from his office relates both to bookselling and publishing. There are two main series of files, one in alphabetical order, c.1960-81, the other a series of publishing files, 1950-81, with a separate file dedicated to individual books or authors. In addition, there are isolated files on assorted subjects, and items of correspondence that have either been preserved separately or removed from files because of their subject matter or authorship. In this last category is correspondence with, among others, George Bernard Shaw, John Betjeman and J.R.R. Tolkien, and letters from T.S. Eliot, Edith Sitwell and Stephen Spender.

Correspondence, c.1919-84

Articles, Essays and Speeches

Throughout his long life and professional career, Basil Blackwell wrote and spoke extensively, and was equally at home addressing a school prize-giving as a professional society, or giving an after-dinner speech. His writing spanned 'the world of books' to the welfare state and penal reform. His speeches and writings survive as off-prints, manuscripts and typescripts.

Articles, essays and speeches, 1929-81; cards used by BB in his talks, n.d.

Legal

Copies of BB's service agreement with B H Blackwell Ltd, as Managing Director, 1963, and as President of the Company, 1969. 1963, 1969

The Book Ring

The 'Book Ring' was an unofficial group of antiquarian booksellers who colluded at auctions of antiquarian books to realise low prices. Books so purchased would be subsequently re-auctioned by the dealers among themselves and eventually sold on for a large profit. As a former President of the International Association of Antiquarian Booksellers, Basil Blackwell took action to restrict this practice, resulting in the resolution that any member in contravention of the Auctions (Bidding Agreements) Act should resign from the Association.

Copy of An Act to render illegal certain agreements and transactions affecting bidding at auctions, Chapter 12 [re book ring], 1927; correspondence and newscuttings, 1955-6; list of "Saints", i.e. booksellers who were not involved with the book ring; counsel's opinion on BB's intended actions re the book ring and draft form of statutory declaration for the "Saints" to sign, 1955; blank copies of the statutory declaration; invoices for costs involved; statutory declarations completed by "Saints", 1955-6; Hansard Parliamentary debates, vol. 557, no.201, Antiquarian Booksellers (Buyers' Ring) Adjournment debate, 27 July 1956; notes on "The Ring", n.d. 1927-56

The International Association of Antiquarian Booksellers

The IAAB, also known as the Antiquarian Booksellers Association, was founded in 1906. Benjamin Blackwell served in the office of President in 1913, and Basil Blackwell served as its President in 1925 and 1926.

Printed annual report, 1926; art work by E.H. New, for the menu for the Association's annual dinner, 1926.

The Classical Association
Basil Blackwell was a longstanding member of the Classical Association and President 1964-5.

Correspondence, 1963-4; programme of the Annual Conference, 1965; galley proofs and printed copies of Presidential Address, *Retreat from Grammar*, given at the University of Manchester, 1965; newscuttings relating to the same; letters of thanks for copies of Presidential Address, 1965. 1963-5

The Johnson Birthplace Museum
Papers re the appeal for the restoration of the Dr Johnson Birthplace Museum in Lichfield, incl. correspondence, 1968-71; copies of printed appeal, 1970; programme of the official re-opening; copy of the menu for the celebratory supper, 1971; newscuttings and letters of thanks, 1971. 1968-71

William Morris Society
Basil Blackwell was a supporter of the work of the William Morris Society for many years, serving as a trustee, and President 1968-79. When the William Morris Centre opened in 1976, Basil Blackwell loaned the Albion hand printing press that had been used by A.H. Bullen at the Shakespeare Head Press in Stratford-upon-Avon, and which was believed to have been used by William Morris to print the Kelmscott Chaucer.

Letter of May Morris, daughter of William Morris, 1932; memoir of May Morris by BB, 1958; article on May Morris by BB, including photograph of May Morris and Mary Lobb, n.d.; information on William Morris Society, 1960; correspondence, 1967-87; correspondence on the publication of *The Story of Kormak the Son of Ogmund* by the William Morris Society, [*The Story of Kormak* was a previously unpublished work by William Morris], 1968-82; papers re the Albion printing press believed to have been used by William Morris at Kelmscott, used later at the Shakespeare Head Press, Stratford, including: photograph of the printing room of the Shakespeare Head Press at Stratford-upon-Avon, n.d., [pre-1920]; article by BB on the history of the Albion printing press; correspondence on the loan of the press to the William Morris Centre, 1971-4; printed leaflets on the William Morris Centre, 1976-7; copy of BB's speech at the opening of the William Morris Centre, 1976; printed copy of the Constitution of the William Morris Society, n.d.; copies of the Society's Newsletter and Journal,1978, 1982 and 1984; papers re Jack Walsdorf, bibliophile and authority on William Morris and the Kelmscott Chaucer, 1980-3; copy of Blackwell's catalogue 929, Kelmscott Press Books; correspondence between BB and Arthur Sanderson and Sons re gift of an original pearwood printing block used for printing William Morris wallpaper, 1971; William Morris pearwood printing block presented to BB by Arthur Sanderson and Sons, 1971; roll of reproduction William Morris wallpaper, handblocked, 1975. 1932-82

Magistracy
Papers re Brian Leighton, J.P, and his promotion of suspended sentences, 1964-7; book containing text of speech/article on prisons and the penal system, n.d.; papers re BB's retirement from the Bench, incl. correspondence, photographs, news cuttings, 1964. 1964-7

FAMILY TREE OF THE BLACKWELL AND RELATED FAMILIES

Joshua BLACKWELL =
m. 1808, St Andrew's, Holbo

John TAYLOR = Sarah RICHES
c.12 October 1805   b. c. 1807
Attleborough, Norfolk   Hingham, Norfolk
m. 15 October 1832

Ann Stirling LAM
1823,

Charlotte   John ('Jack')   Lydia ('Lilla') TAYLOR = Benjamin Henry BLACKWELL
b. c.1848   b. 1849, Oxford
Hingham, Norfolk   m. 26 August 1886
d. 1927   d. 26 October 1924

Dorothy Stirling = Sumner AUSTIN
b. 1887   b. 24 September 1888
m. 1921
d. 1979   d. 9 July 1981

Richard = Marguerite HOLLIDAY   Helen = Donald BUTCHER   Penelope = Robert JESSE
b. 1918
m. 1942
d. 1980

Miles   Nigel   Adam   Rosalind   Max   Stephen   David

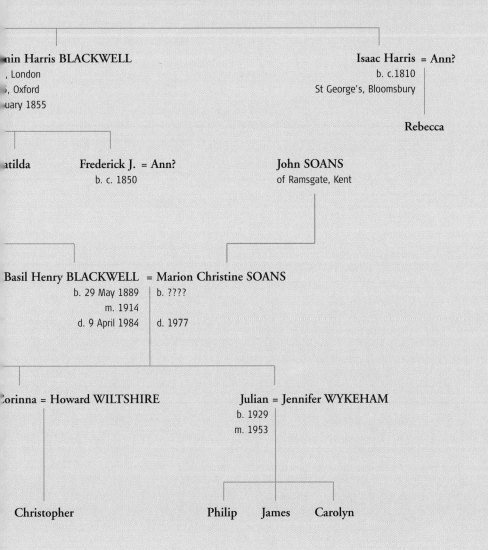

...nin Harris BLACKWELL
, London
, Oxford
...uary 1855

Isaac Harris = Ann?
b. c.1810
St George's, Bloomsbury

Rebecca

...atilda

Frederick J. = Ann?
b. c. 1850

John SOANS
of Ramsgate, Kent

Basil Henry BLACKWELL = Marion Christine SOANS
b. 29 May 1889   b. ????
m. 1914
d. 9 April 1984   d. 1977

...orinna = Howard WILTSHIRE

Julian = Jennifer WYKEHAM
b. 1929
m. 1953

Christopher

Philip   James   Carolyn

Miscellaneous

Copy of BB's poem, *Brian and Estoile*, 1907; papers and printed material re BB as expert witness in the *Last Exit to Brooklyn* obscenity trial, 1966; news cuttings by or about BB; news cuttings about B H Blackwell's; material for BB's entry for John Gideon Wilson (1876-1963) in the *Supplement of the Dictionary of National Biography*, c.1963; samples of BB's visiting card and compliment slips; papers re Dorothy L. Sayers, incl. copies of correspondence, reviews of biographies, and newscuttings, c.1916-81

Richard Blackwell (The Guv'nor)

Richard Blackwell joined the business of B H Blackwell Ltd. in 1946, becoming managing director in 1956 and chairman in 1969. He was chairman of Basil Blackwell Publisher Ltd. (formerly Basil Blackwell and Mott Ltd.) from 1976 until his death in 1980. Papers in the collection are limited to a small quantity of correspondence, a number of articles and texts of speeches, and newspaper cuttings.

Correspondence

Correspondence, labelled "interesting letters", 1968-80; correspondence with Barr Smith Library, University of Adelaide, 1941-75; correspondence with various universities, soliciting information for the company history, c.1978. 1968-80

Articles and Speeches

'The Day's Bag in a Bookshop', reprint of article by RB from *The Journal of Industrial Economics*, Vol. IX, No.1, Nov.1960; typescript article by RB on history of B H Blackwell Ltd, 1963; tape recording and typescript of address by RB to National Library Training School, 1967; copy of speech by RB to International Group of Scientific, Technical and Medical Publishers, 1974; copy of speech by RB at South African Bibliophiles' Conference, 1978; copy of interview by RB with *Oxford Mail and Times* in "Men at the Top" series; 'Examination of the Net Book Agreement', typescript by RB, n.d. 1960-78

Miles Blackwell

Correspondence

Personal and business correspondence, 1979-89; letters of congratulations on becoming chairman of B H Blackwell Ltd, 1982; letters of thanks from people who received a copy of the history of the firm, 1983; letters of condolence to and replies from MB on death of Sir Basil Blackwell, 1984; correspondence with Professor Tscha Hung (alias Hong Qian), Professor of Philosophy at Beijing University, and with his widow and colleagues after his death, 1984-92; copy of obituary of Professor Tscha Hung in *The Independent*, 20 March 1992

Foreign contacts and business trips

Small quantity of ephemera re trip to Japan, 1981; papers re trade visits to China, incl. photographs, ephemera and visitors books for conference dinners hosted in Beijing, also photographs of Chinese delegations to Blackwell's shop in Oxford, 1984-9; copies of contracts between the Special Book Acquisition Fund Department [SPAFD], State Education Commission, People's Republic of China, and B H Blackwell Ltd; and SPAFD and Blackwell North America; photographs of the signing of the contracts, 1986

Papers, e.g. invitations, itineraries, news cuttings and photographs, re overseas visits and information on overseas contacts, incl. Australia, New Zealand, South Africa, Nigeria, United States of America, Canada and Singapore, 1979-93

Miscellaneous
Cards congratulating MB on 18th and 20th anniversaries of joining the firm; samples of "Blessing of the Eid" cards sent by MB, 1979-88; news cuttings by and about MB and B H Blackwell's, c.1979-89; ephemera relating to ceremonies, dinners, commemoration services etc., 1989-93; promotional literature on the University of Regina, Canada, 1989; *In Transit: Sydney CAE, 1982-1989*, printed history of Sydney College of Advanced Education, 1989

Chairman's Office, Celebrations

Centenary of the Company
The centenary of the company was celebrated with a thanksgiving service and lunch in Merton College in January 1979, and further celebrations at Blenheim Palace and Trinity College.

Papers re celebrations at Merton College, 3 January 1979, incl. thanksgiving service and lunch in hall, January 1979; papers re parties at Blenheim Palace and Trinity College, 1979; photographs of centenary parties at Trinity College, Blenheim Palace and Fyfield Manor, 1979; letter re dinner given by Barclays Bank for centenary, 1979; two printing plates used in centenary edition of *Broad Sheet*,1979; news cuttings, centenary editions of the *Broad Sheet,* 'regret unable to accept' letters, 1979.

Centenary, Company History
A published history of the company was envisaged as an integral part of the centenary celebrations. Much information was supplied by Sir Basil Blackwell, who had long been prevailed upon to write his memoirs, as well as by long-serving members of the company. Some of the memoirs supplied by the latter are to be found among the records of staff. Further information was also solicited from longstanding customers, such as overseas university libraries. The history was written by Sir Arthur Norrington, a former President of Trinity College, and was published in 1983.

Memorandum by Richard Blackwell on projected history of Blackwell's,1976; drafts of text; various comments on text; memoranda; correspondence with Sir Arthur Norrington; background information solicited from former customers, e.g. university librarians, 1977-81; typescript of the *History of Blackwell, 1879-1979 – Part II*, n.d.; articles on the Churchman's Union Building and Bliss Court, [possibly for company history], n.d.; unexpurgated draft of *Blackwell's, 1879-1979*, with file of reviews and 'thank you' letters, 1983.

The Restoration of the Muses, Clarendon Building
The 'Muses' are the statues of Melpomene and Euterpe on the parapet of the Clarendon Building, originally erected in 1717. One of them collapsed in 1897 and the other in about 1912. In 1973, Blackwell's undertook to replace the statues, working from sketches in Worcester College Library. The replacements were made by Richard Kindersley in reinforced glass fibre with a resin-lead finish, and officially unveiled on 6 June 1974.

Correspondence; invitation card to the unveiling of the statues and celebration concert; order of proceedings; 'thank you' letters for the party; accounts for the two statues and party; copy of article in *Broad Sheet*, June 1974; photographs; news cuttings. 1973-4

Gaffer's 90th Birthday

Sir Basil Blackwell's 90th birthday was celebrated by the publication of a series of essays titled *Boethius: his life, thought and influence,* edited by Margaret Gibson. The essays were published in 1981, and celebrated with a party in the Norrington Room on 29 October 1981.

Invitation; typescript account of the order of proceedings; card from Margaret Gibson; cassette tape of the Boethius celebrations; autographs of guests attending the party; letters of thanks and comment; literary reviews of Margaret Gibson's *Boethius*; background papers to publication; account for expenses incurred; printed essays and articles on Boethius, 1936-81

Other Celebrations

Papers re various events celebrated by the company, incl. menus; guest lists; correspondence; seating plans; photographs, etc. Events incl. return of staff serving in the Second World War; 50th, 75th and 90th anniversaries of the company; retirement dinner for Sir Arthur Norrington, 1970; and "Old Guard" dinner, 1972. 1946-72

Chairman's Office, Miscellaneous

Petition against an early form of Net Book Agreement containing, "signatures of Persons attending Meeting of Writers in Support of John Chapman's campaign", 4 May 1852; obituaries of friends of the firm, 1950-85; articles and press cuttings on Oxford, 1923-88; photographs, incl. late 19th cent. stereoscopic photographs of Oxford,

Signatories to petition "in Support of John Chapman's campaign against the Booksellers Association" include Charles Dickens and Wilkie Collins, 1852

photographs of the Sheldonian Theatre before and after restoration, and the heads of the Caesars after replacement, 1972; samples of Blackwell's "emergency mail service" stamps, n.d.; correspondence re gifts made by B H Blackwell Ltd. to universities, principally gifts of rare books on special anniversaries, acquisition of 1 millionth book, etc. 1979-90

B H Blackwell's Bookshop

Benjamin Henry Blackwell opened his bookshop at 50 Broad Street on 1 January 1879. The business was incorporated as a Limited Liability Company on 11 March 1920.

Corporate records
Printed memorandum and articles of association, 1920; directors' minute books, 1920-60, 1964-5; Thursday Meeting (from 1969, Managing Directors' Weekly Meeting) minute books, 1930-75; Booksellers' Committee minute books, 1968-76; papers re setting up of Specialists' Committee, 1972-3, and minutes, 1974-6

Financial records
IOUs from Benjamin Henry Blackwell to various individuals, 1879-89; invoice of account of E.J. Withington of Balliol with B.H. Blackwell, 1882; bills and vouchers, late 19th and early 20th cents.; correspondence re Income Tax, 1905; private ledgers, 1907-16, 1924-8; stock accounts, 1920, 1921; monthly sales analysis books, 1930-67, 1972-84; annual statements of account (some years missing), 1899-1980; publication department profit and loss accounts, 1913, 1915, 1918

Customer records
Memorandum from Benjamin Henry Blackwell to Miss G. James re book order, 1907; purchases and sales ledgers, 1929-32, 1938-43, 1947-58; mailing list with receipt from Barclay's Bank, High Street, Oxford, for deposit of the same, 15 January 1941; records of individuals trying to sell stolen books to Blackwell's, incl. reports, memoranda and news cuttings, 1954-71.

Broad Street

Property records
Sun Fire Office insurance policy on 51 Broad Street, 16 September 1842; printed sale particulars of dwelling house on Broad Street, 1860; draft agreement between Mr B.H. Blackwell and Miss M.A. Lockwood on tenancy of 51 Broad Street, June 1885; mortgage between B.H. Blackwell and Mrs Teresa Messer, on tenement in Broad Street, 25 April 1883; schedule of deeds of 50-51 Broad Street, and 1 Linton Road, n.d.; correspondence with Trinity College re Churchmans Union Building, 1892-7; letter from BB to the President of Trinity College re possible purchase of Bliss Court cottages and 48-49 Broad Street, 6 March 1923

Norrington Room
An underground extension to Blackwell's Bookshop was proposed by Julian Blackwell in 1962. The room was designed by Robert Maguire and Keith Murray with a floor space of 10,000 square feet. It was named after Sir Arthur Norrington, then President of Trinity College, and formally opened in 1966. Murals celebrating significant characters and events in the life of Oxford, to decorate the entrance stairwell, were commissioned of the artist Edward Bawden in 1969 and completed in 1973.

Photographs of the Norrington Room, under construction, 1964, on completion, 1966, and book sales, 1981, 1984; papers re opening of the Norrington Room incl. blank invitations, photographs, copy of Trinity College magazine, with article on Norrington Room, *Report of Trinity College,* Adam Fox's poem about the Norrington Room, news cuttings, 1966; correspondence with Edward Bawden and Ruari McLean on the commissioning of the Norrington Room

*First entry in
Directors' Minute
Book, 22 March 1920*

mural, 1969-73; Edward Bawden's cartoons for the Norrington Room mural, c.1973; black and white photographs of Edward Bawden at work on the Norrington Room mural, c.1973; photographs of the Norrington Room mural, with identifying key, 1973; papers re unveiling of Norrington Room mural, incl. invitations, photographs and news cuttings, 1973; *The World of Edward Bawden:* catalogue of an exhibition of the work of Edward Bawden at the Ashmolean Museum, January-February 1974

Pictures and Photographs

A large number of photographs of Blackwell's shop have survived, from c.1890-1986. These include black and white and colour photographs, of both the exterior and interior of the shop. They also include general views of the shop as well as views of the Churchman's Union Building, specialist departments, e.g. Theology, Science and Classics, and the Gaffer's Room; engraving of Muirhead Bone's pastel drawing of the interior of Blackwell's, with explanation, 1950

Broad Street, Miscellaneous

The Recently Demolished Houses in Broad Street, Oxford, article by W.A. Pantin, reprinted from *Oxoniensia* Vol. II (1937), with accompanying letter from W.A. Pantin, Oriel College, 3 February 1938; visitors' book, 1960-96; account of visit by Paul Verlaine to Blackwell's shop, n.d.

Marketing

Advertisement for "B.H. Blackwell" from *The Oxford Magazine,* 21 October 1885; proofs of coloured postcards reproducing 18th and 19th cent. engravings of views of Oxford, n.d.; samples of Christmas cards sent to customers by B H Blackwell Ltd., c.1948-87;

photographs, news cuttings and copies of *Broad Sheet* articles re book signings and literary lunches, 1972-87; correspondence re displays in Blackwell's bookshop, c.1980; copies of Blackwell's *Marketing Bulletin*, May-September 1988; postcards of front of Blackwell's shop, 50 Broad Street, n.d.; samples of bookmarks, posters and paperbags.

Catalogues

Benjamin Henry Blackwell published his first catalogue of second-hand and antiquarian books to coincide with the opening of his shop in January 1879. New books first appeared alongside second-hand books in the Educational catalogues in 1887, a catalogue of books for the general reader appeared in time for the Christmas market in 1894 and an 'advance impression' for the American market in 1896. Specialist catalogues were produced in increasingly diverse fields including Classics, History, Theology, Science and Medicine, reflecting the growth in both the retail and publishing sides of the business. Catalogue No. 1 was reprinted in 1973 to coincide with the issue of the firm's catalogue No. 1000.

Individual printed general book catalogues in a numbered sequence up to c.1200, most in binders. c.1950-c.1985

Individual printed rare book catalogues, most marked up with who bought the books and purchase price, c.1950-c.1985

Children's Bookshops

The Children's Bookshop was opened at 22 Broad Street in 1950. Outgrowing these premises, it moved to 6 Broad Street in 1974, and later returned to the main shop at 48-51 Broad Street.

Interior of the Churchman's Union Building, at the rear of Blackwell's, c 1930s

Photographs, incl. children's Christmas parties, 1978-9, 1981, 1984, Children's Book Fair, 1978, 1982, 1984, and television artist Tony Hart , 1984; miscellaneous articles re Children's Book Shop taken from *Broad Sheet*, 1987, 1988

Music Bookshop

A music department was established in B H Blackwell's under Frederick Dymond in the early 1950s and moved to separate premises next to the King's Arms, Holywell Street, in 1955. A purpose-built shop was opened next to the existing premises by Sir Adrian Boult in 1970. It was later transferred to a more central site at 23-25 Broad Street, facing Blackwell's main shop.

Correspondence re establishment of the music shop and the opening of the new

A selection of Blackwell's book catalogues

music shop, 1955-72; photographs, incl. the old and new music shops, n.d. [pre and post 1970], the opening of the new music shop by Sir Adrian Boult, 1970, party at the music shop to celebrate the publication of the *New Grove Dictionary of Music*, 1981, lute and guitar recitals at the music shop, 1985; printing plate for the invitation to the opening of the new music shop, 1970; article on the new music shop from *The Daily Telegraph*, 4 December 1971; advertising ephemera, n.d.

Antiquarian Books Department

Invoices, 1925-51; binding orders receipt book, 1937-51; catalogues of Sotheby's rare books sales, 1947-1978; purchases and sales books, 1948-1951, 1958, 1962-82; correspondence re purchase at auction and subsequent sale of a set of autographs of American Presidents, 1964-5; correspondence with customers re sales and purchases, 1968-72; "The Black Booke of Shippe Street", containing photographs that convinced Richard Blackwell the Antiquarian Department should be moved from the Ship Street premises, c.1975; papers re acquisition of Fyfield Manor as Antiquarian Department, incl. sales particulars and floor plan, c.1979; photographs, artwork and correspondence with Barry Moser re engraving of Fyfield Manor, 1979; 2 printing blocks of Fyfield Manor, one of engraving by Barry Moser, the other a wood engraving by Richard Parker, c.1979; proof of headed notepaper for Antiquarian Department, Fyfield, 1979; correspondence between Peter Fenemore and Morrell, Peel and Gamlen re valuation for probate of the manuscripts and literary papers of J.R.R. Tolkien; copies of posters for Blackwell's new Antiquarian Department, Fyfield, 1979; notes on the history of Fyfield Manor with artwork, possibly for printed promotional literature, c.1980; visitors books, 1979-91; miscellaneous papers sent to archives formerly housed at Fyfield incl. copy of *Juvenilia*, magazine produced by pupils of King's College, Wimbledon, Issue 1, 11

February 1833; manuscript volume of poems by John Gawsworth, from the library of John Masefield, 1943; invitation to Mrs John Masefield to Royal Garden Party, 1947; letter to Mrs Masefield, 1942; letters from T.S. Eliot at Faber and Faber to H.W. Garrod, Merton College, re gift to Merton College of a manuscript by George Saintsbury, 1948-9; letters to John Masefield, 1953; news cuttings re book auctions and prices realised, many purchased by Blackwell's, 1960s and 1970s

Beaver House

By the middle of the 1960s, the greater part of the company's business came from mail order sales, including UK mail order, export and periodicals. A report produced in 1967 recommended the bringing together under one roof of the various distribution departments and the Accounts Division. The new headquarters, Beaver House, was opened in 1973.

Distribution
Correspondence and catalogues re purchase of a delivery van, 1909-12; bicycle catalogue, 1912; photographs of Blackwell's delivery vans, c.1950

Mail Order Division
Memoranda and consultation documents relating to the revival and reorganisation of the Mail Order Division, 1978-9

Accounts Department
Photographs, c.1950-65; summaries of results, B H Blackwell Ltd, 1920-77

Blanket Orders Department
Printed information on service, n.d., c.1970; photograph, 1974; consultation documents, n.d., c.1975;

Mail Order Department/New Books System
Information leaflets and copies of articles in *Broad Sheet*; photographs, c.1960-75

Periodical Department
Photographs, c.1950-85; report on departmental reorganisation, c.1965; promotional literature on service, c.1975-85; notes on the Periodical Department for company history, c.1979; photographs of Hythe Bridge Street before the building of Beaver House; photographs of the outside of Beaver House and of the topping out ceremony by, 1973; photographs of Beaver House incl. boiler room, c.1975, and computer room, 1978-79

Switchboard
Photographs of the old and new switchboards at Broad Street and Beaver House, n.d., c.1970-85; article on the switchboard from *Broad Sheet*, 1987

Staff records
Papers re company Profit Sharing Scheme, 1913-16; staff pension scheme account book, 1916-30; staff address book kept by Eleanor Halliday, Basil Blackwell's secretary, c.1946; typed list of company staff, n.d., c.1960; *Instructions for Chargers* and *Instructions for Correspondence Departments*, typescript, 1966; *General Instructions (Shop Staff Bible)*, n.d., c.1968; printed copies of *Staff Rules and*

Blackwell's apprentices with 'delivery' quadracycle

Conditions, 1967, 1974, post 1978; printed *B H Blackwell Ltd. Staff Rules and Policy Handbook,* n.d.; printed details of Blackwell's Superannuation Fund, 1970; illustrated brochures on careers at Blackwell's, c.1972; *Blackwell's Staff Association Constitution and Rules,* n.d. [c.1975]; personal memoir by Gladys Roby about Blackwell's staff, n.d.[?1978]; company organisation charts, 1981; Personnel Department photographs, 1980-1; article on Personnel Department from *Broad Sheet,* 1987

Directors

Material re Blackwell's directors, incl. photographs, copies of articles in *Broad Sheet,* news cuttings, invitations and menus for celebratory dinners, and autobiographical notes, 1883-1988

Directors represented incl. Peter Bagnell, Geoffrey Barfoot, Sir John Brown, George Bunting, John Cutforth, Charles Field, Christopher Francis, Frederick Hanks, R.Hillier, Edgar Hine, William Hunt, Will King, Harry Knights, John Merriman, Sir Adrian Mott, Cecil Palmer, Ernest Wilfred Parker, Herbert Steele, Fred Stevens, David Young and C.P. Wareham.

Individual Members of Staff

Material re individual members of staff, incl. photographs, copies of articles in *Broad Sheet,* news cuttings and autobiographical notes, c.1890-1989

Staff represented incl. Joan Baskerville, Fred Chaundy, Edward East, H.G. Gadney, George Innes, Reggie Nash and Reginald Sherbourn.

The Blackwellians: Amateur Dramatic Society

The Blackwellians amateur dramatic society was founded in 1948, and debuted with Noel Coward's *This Happy Breed.*

Programmes signed by the cast, albums of photographs of productions, copies of scripts and press reviews of productions, 1948-53

Sports and Social Club

Invitation to staff party, 1938; photographs of company and society events, incl. sports matches, Miss Blackwell competition, 1971, Christmas parties, and long-service and retirement parties, c.1948-85; papers re staff outings to annual Oxford and Cambridge Universities Rugby match, Twickenham, 1954-79; programmes for annual Oxford and Cambridge Universities Rugby match, 1954-72, 1974-7, 1981

Not So Young Club

The Not So Young Club was founded for retired staff of B H Blackwell in 1979.

Newsletters; Action Committee minutes; completed membership application forms for the founding year; correspondence, 1978-87; invitation to and photogaphs of the Not So Young Club's party for Gaffer's 90th birthday, 1979; invitation from Mrs Richard Blackwell to members of the Not So Young Club to a tea at Fyfield Manor to celebrate the 10th anniversary of the Club, 1989; albums of photographs of Not So Young Club parties, c.1980

Broad Sheet – staff newsletter

The staff newsletter, *Broad Sheet*, was introduced as a short newsletter of 1-2 pages of typescript in September 1946, to inform staff of events within the firm, new arrivals and departures of staff, and so on. It adopted a broadsheet format, including photographs, in February 1971. Significant events, such as the centenary of the firm and Gaffer's 90th birthday, have been commemorated by the production of special editions of *Broad Sheet*.

Broad Sheet, 1946-88; photographs used in *Broad Sheet*, annotated with month of issue and subject, 1981-8

Blackwell's takes to the Boards

Blackwellians at play: Hockey Match, c.1950

Basil Blackwell Publishing (formerly Basil Blackwell and Mott)

Benjamin Henry Blackwell commenced publishing from the outset, producing his first catalogue to coincide with opening of his shop on 1 January 1879. A small volume, *Mensae Secundae: Verses written in Balliol*, appeared in the same year. He published further catalogues, as well as limited impressions of student poetry and prize essays. After a year with Oxford University Press in London, Basil Blackwell joined the family firm in 1913 to run the publishing department. In 1922, he founded the separate publishing company of Basil Blackwell and Mott with Adrian Mott, an old college friend. The name of the company was changed to Basil Blackwell Publishing in 1978.

Corporate records

Certificate of incorporation, 1922; memoranda and articles of association, 1922, 1961; articles of association, Blackwell Scientific Publications, 1939; financial reports on the credit-worthiness of Blackwell and Mott, c.1913-27; correspondence, memoranda and reports re various aspects of Blackwell and Mott/Basil Blackwell Publishing, e.g. sales, lists of titles for destruction or discontinuation, books for publication, etc., c.1963-84

Financial records

Annual statements of account, 1960-77; Blackwell Scientific Publications annual statements of account, 1940-59, 1980-1

Miscellaneous

News cuttings, incl. reviews of books published by Blackwell and Mott, 1932-70; information on Blackwell's Junior Poetry Books series, 1960; negatives and proofs of photographs of Basil Blackwell Publishing party, Fyfield, 1980; first edition of *Oxford Today* magazine, published by Basil Blackwell Publishing, 1988; typed notes on Blackwell and Mott, annotated, n.d.; typescript notes by R.H. Sherbourn for the history of Blackwell and Mott Ltd, n.d.

Allied Businesses and Subsidiaries

Parkers of Broad Street

Parker and Son (later Parkers) of Broad Street traces its origins to the business of Joseph Fletcher, bookseller, established in 1731. The founder of the company's name, Sackville Parker, had premises at the corner of Logic Lane in the 1780s. After a period with James Robson of New Bond Street, London, his nephew, Joseph Parker, went into partnership with Fletcher and Hanwell of Broad Street in 1797. James Fletcher died in 1802 and his widow, Elizabeth, in 1816, when Joseph Parker continued to run the business until his retirement in 1832. He was succeeded in turn by his nephew, John Henry Parker, who was a publisher of Keble, Pusey and others of the Oxford Movement . John Parker retired in 1862, succeeded first by his son, James, and his grandson, Charles John Parker, in 1912. The business was incorporated as a Limited Liability Company in 1927. Charles Parker died in 1930 and, in the absence of any heirs, the business was conducted by trustees until B H Blackwell acquired half of the business in 1937, on the understanding that it preserve its own identity. Its premises at 26-27 Broad Street were taken over as Blackwell's Art and Poster Shop during the 1980s.

Corporate records

Articles of partnership, Fletcher, Hanwell and Parker, 1797; articles of association, Parker and Son, Ltd., 1927; printed memorandum and articles of association of Parker and Son Ltd., 1927; certificate of incorporation, 1927; draft dividend list, 1936; shares tender, 1938.

Financial records

Cash books, 1911-64; Barclays Bank Pass Book, 1913-24; balance sheets book, 1927-33; annual statements of account, 1937-40, 1944-5, 1948-52, 1954-9, 1970, 1972-81; sales reports, 1958-71

Customer records

Sales ledgers, 1794-1800, 1908-1964; standing orders books, 1900-54; stock receipt book, 1897-1926; account book of sales to and purchases from Thornton's bookshop, Broad Street, Oxford,1967-75; letter to Parker's from Davies and Son of Gloucester re purchase of books, 1855

Staff records

Wages books, 1864-1961; Staff Rules and Conditions of Employment, 1972

Property records

Lease of 27 Broad Street, 21 Turl Street, 26 Broad Street (part), with inventories, rating assessment, 1926-52

Marketing records

Catalogues, c.1852-1911, 1981-83; black and white photographs of Parker's, marked up as artwork for one of Parker's 'Publications for Libraries'; advertising bookmarks, n.d.

Account of Rev. Scrope Berdmore, Warden of Merton, with Fletcher and Hanwell, 1796

Letter from Sackville Parker to John Nourse, bookseller, Strand, London, 1758

Family

Family tree of the Parker family, n.d.;
biographies of members of the Parker family;
photograph of James Parker, n.d., [c.1900];
photograph of Mrs Parker, n.d., [c.1900]

Miscellaneous

Letter from Sackville Parker, 1758; prints of
Turl Street, 1782-1880; plans of occupiers of
Parker's site c.1780 and post 1788, n.d.;
visitors' book, early 1980s; photographs of
staff and premises, c.1970, c.1980s; a
pictorial envelope sent to Parker's,
December, 1881, with newspaper article re
same, 1987; notes on the history of Parker
and Son Ltd., n.d.; Parker's "Reject" desk
stamp; photographs of documents and
pictures associated with Parker's, n.d.

William George's Sons Ltd, Bristol

William George opened his book shop in 16
Bath Street, Bristol, in 1847, having first served
his apprenticeship at the business of William
Strong, 26 Clare Street. He issued his first
catalogue in 1848 and moved his shop to 28
Bath Street in 1850. The shop moved again, in
1871, to 26 Park Street, and finally, in 1878, to
89 Park Street. William George enrolled his two
sons, Charles William and Frank, as partners in
1884 and gradually took a less active role in
the business until his death in 1900. The
younger partner, Frank George, died in 1905
and the business was converted to a Limited
Liability Company in 1924. In declining health,
Charles George entered into negotiations with
B H Blackwell, who acquired the controlling
share of the business in 1929, continuing to
run the shop as a separate business. Charles
George died in 1935.

Corporate records

Articles of association, 1924, 1959; papers
re takeover of William George's Sons by
B H Blackwell, 1929; letter from Margaret
Thorn to BB on the future of the business,
1935; personal and business correspondence
between BB and others relating to William
George's Bookshop,1956-79;
correspondence, reports, etc., re shares in
William George's Sons Ltd and George's
Bookshop (Exeter) Ltd., c.1985-8

Financial records

Cash sales ledger, 1928-54; annual
statements of accounts, 1930, 1938-77,
1988; business reports, 1934, 1936-7, 1942,
1944-5; report on the George's Group
accounts department, 1987

Miscellaneous

Leaflet on the centenary of William George's
Sons Ltd., 1947; news cuttings re party to
celebrate opening of new extension to
William George's Sons Ltd. bookshop, 1964;
miscellaneous news cuttings, 1964-6; printed
and typescript material on the history of the
firm, n.d.

Alden and Blackwell (Eton)

Articles of association, 1946; notice of first
Annual General Meeting, 1947;
correspondence re Alden Press/Alden and
Blackwell, 1945-7; annual statements of
account, 1947-51, 1953-62, 1964-8, 1970,
1972-7

Davenant Bookshop, Oxford

The Davenant Bookshop was acquired from H.G. Gadney in 1922, with Gadney continuing as manager. It transferred to 41 High Street in 1930 and continued in existence until the expiry of its lease in 1938.

Purchases and sales account book, 1923-35

Paperback Shop, Oxford

Annual statements of accounts, 1963-72

Stone's Bookshop Ltd.

Annual statements of account, 1973-7

Turl Cash Bookshop, Oxford

The Turl Cash Bookshop opened in Turl Street following the removal of the Davenant Bookshop to 41 High Street in 1930.

Annual statements of accounts, 1947-63, 1965-8

University Bookshop (Exeter) Ltd

Annual statements of account, 1972-7

F. A. Wood's Bookshop, Broad Street, Oxford

Invoice for purchase of Wood's stock by B H Blackwell, 1940; annual statements of account, 1946-59; draft balance sheets and profit and loss accounts, 1949, 1951

Shakespeare Head Press

A.H. Bullen founded the Shakespeare Head Press (SHP) at 21 Chapel Street, Stratford-upon-Avon, in 1904 with the express intention of producing the first edition of the complete works of Shakespeare to be printed in his home town. This appeared in 1907 as the *Stratford Town Shakespeare*. The early history of the project is recorded in the diary kept by his business partner, Frank Sidgwick, between May 1904 and March 1905. Unfortunately, Bullen was no businessman and by the time of his death in 1919 the Press was virtually bankrupt. Basil Blackwell purchased the Press in 1921 with the intention of producing fine books, with the assistance of the typographer Bernard Newdigate. Among the works produced by the SHP are the works of Froissart (1927-28), Chaucer (1928-29), Spenser (1930), Malory's *Morte Darthur* (1935) and a single-volume Shakespeare (1935). Blackwell and Mott (B & M) were appointed publishers to SHP in 1922, and the Press was relocated from Stratford to 33 St Aldate's, Oxford, in May 1930 to simplify production. The financial recession of the 1930s reduced sales of fine books and the presses were partly turned over to the production of educational books for B & M. The St Aldate's premises were requisitioned for war purposes in 1942 and the plant sold, when the Press became, in effect, a subsidiary department of B & M.

Corporate records

Articles of association, 1921; directors' minute book, 1925-63

*A selection of
Shakespeare Head
Press material*

Financial records
Nominal Ledger, 1930-57; annual statements
of accounts, 1925-65, 1967-77

Production records
Printing blocks from SHP edition of Froissart's
Chronicles; woodblocks from SHP edition of
Boccaccio's *Decameron*; copper printing plate,
showing open volume of Richardson's *Pamela*;
samples of fine printing by the SHP, c.1930-9

Staff records
Personal diary of Frank Sidgwick, recording
the setting up of the SHP at Stratford-upon-
Avon with A.H. Bullen, 1904-5; photograph
of Frank Sidgwick, n.d.; black and white
photographs of the SHP in Stratford as
illustrations for the publication of the diary;
prospectus for published edition of Frank
Sidgwick's Diary ; biographical notes on John
Farleigh, wood engraver, who worked for the
SHP, n.d.

Marketing
Promotional booklet on SHP, 1904;
prospectus for the *Stratford Town
Shakespeare*, 1907; prospectuses for the
SHP editions of Froissart's *Chronicles*, 1928
and Mallory's *Morte Darthur*, 1933;
advertising lists of SHP publications, 1915,
1921, 1929, 1939

Miscellaneous
Menu for SHP dinner at Simpsons of the
Strand, 1907; visitors' book, 1911-39;
correspondence between P. Lister and M.H.
Spielmann relating to SHP following the
death of A.H.Bullen, 1920; article on the SHP
by BB from *The Bookman's Journal*,
December 1921; articles by Bernard
Newdigate on the SHP, 1931 and fine
printing, 1935; news cuttings about SHP,
c.1934-75; *The Shakespeare Head Press*,
Gordon Bettridge, Manchester, June 1969:
project for "Scholastic Studies in Printing"

course, with letter from Bettridge, 1975; *The University-The Library: papers presented on the occasion of the dedication of the Scott Library*, Shakespeare Head Press, 1972; catalogue of an exhibition of SHP books by A.H. Bullen and Bernard Newdigate at Manchester Polytechnic Library, 1988; texts of speeches/articles by BB on Bernard Newdigate, n.d.

Ovenell and Fowles Bindery

Benjamin Henry Blackwell first went into partnership with Ovenell and Fowles bindery in 1900, but it was formerly acquired by Basil Blackwell and Mott after the incorporation of that company in 1922. Originally based in Wadham Place, Holywell, it later transferred to 5 Alfred Street. It was amalgamated with other binderies to form the Kemp Hall Bindery in 1939 and moved to 33 St Aldate's after WWII.

Annual statements of account, 1908-46

Morley Brothers Bindery

Originally at 16 Longwall Street, the Morley Brothers Bindery was acquired by Basil Blackwell and Mott in 1926. It was amalgamated with other binderies to form Kemp Hall Bindery in 1939 and moved to 33 St Aldate's after WWII.

Private ledger, 1926-44; annual statements of account, 1962-7, 1969-72

Kemp Hall Bindery

Formed by the amalgamation of Ovenell and Fowles, Morley Brothers, Hayes, and W.T. Brown, binderies in 1939. Moved to 33 St Aldate's after WWII.

Annual statements of accounts, 1960, 1964-7, 1970, 1972

J. F. Blakey Ltd.

Annual statements of account, 1969-77

U.P. Jenkins Ltd.

U.P. Jenkins Ltd. was founded in the 1960s as a Management Company in response to perceived governmental interference in internal business management.

Annual statements of accounts, 1970-5, 1977; contracts of employment, 1986-8

Ejnar Munksgaard, Denmark

Annual reports and accounts, 1980-5

Kooyker Scientific Publications

Annual reports and accounts, 1978-84

Outside Organisations

Association of Booksellers of Great Britain and Ireland (ABGBI)

The Association of Booksellers of Great Britain and Ireland was founded in 1895 with the express object of putting an end to the issue of underselling. The Oxford and District Branch was founded in 1899 with Benjamin Henry Blackwell as a founder member. He served the Branch in turn as Secretary and Chairman, and later served on the National Council. He declined the Presidency of the Association in 1924 due to deteriorating health. Basil, Richard and Julian Blackwell all served on the National Council, Basil as President 1934-6, Richard 1966-8 and Julian in 1980. William Hunt, a director of Blackwell's from 1920 to 1939, also served the Oxford Branch as Secretary and later Chairman.

Black and white photograph of the ABGBI conference in Oxford, 1906; letter from BB on behalf of the Associated Booksellers of Great Britain and Ireland, 1940; printed copy of *Objects and Rules of the Booksellers Association of Great Britain and Ireland*, 1983.

Oxford and District Branch:
Executive Committee minute books, 1899-1949; agendas and minutes of Annual General Meetings; agendas of council meetings and reports of council members; financial reports, 1981-7.

The Blackwell Family

Benjamin Harris Blackwell

Copy of *British and Foreign Temperance Intelligencer*, incl. a report on the teetotal activities of B.H. Blackwell, 6 July 1839; photocopy of poster for a lecture on the ill-effects of alcohol c.1840; letter from John Wells to Arthur Norrington, re Benjamin Harris Blackwell as City Librarian, 1977; photocopies from *Oxoniensia*, 1979: article on libraries in Oxford before 1914; photocopy of photograph of gravestone of Benjamin Harris Blackwell in Holywell Cemetery, Oxford, n.d.; packet of book plates inscribed, "Presented to the Oxford Public Library in memory of its First Librarian by his two sons, Nov. 1895"; *Oxford City Librarians, 1854-1954*, n.d.; typescript description of Benjamin Henry Blackwell by BB, n.d.

Ann Stirling (Lambert) Blackwell

Photocopy of letter from George Routledge, 2 Farringdon Street, to Ann Stirling Blackwell, following the death of her husband [Benjamin Harris Blackwell], 1856; black and white photograph of Ann Stirling Blackwell (nee Lambert), wife of Benjamin Harris Blackwell, n.d. [19th cent.]; printed leaflet about the Nancy Stirling Lambert Scholarship Trust, n.d.

Benjamin Henry Blackwell

Personal diaries, 1877-8, 1880-4; black and white studio portrait taken in Dublin, n.d. [late 19th cent.]; invitation to attend the Chamberlain's Court, London Guildhall, to be admitted to the Stationers' Company, 1920; papers re allotment holders in Davenant Road Allotments, 1923; letter from BHB to W. B.[?],

17 July 192[?]; black and white print of St
Placida with illuminated border painted by
BHB, n.d.; *Oxford, City of Spires*, (guidebook
to Oxford, written by BHB), n.d.; obituaries,
news cuttings, letters of condolence, and
orders of funeral service, 1924; list of assets
at date of death, 1924; papers re the estate
of BHB, incl. insurance documents, list of
legatees, 1924; biographical notes on BHB by
his son, Basil Blackwell, 1975, and daughter,
Dorothy Austin, n.d.; photograph of BHB and
Charles Parker, n.d.

Basil Blackwell

Letter from BB to his mother, n.d. [annotated
'Bridlington, 1900'], and letter to William
Griffin from "B.H. Blackwell", 9th January [no
year]; two letters to BB from Christine
Blackwell, 28 Augusta Road, Ramsgate, 1919;
personal diary, c.1939; [autobiographical?]
notes on "Basil Blackwell, Publisher",
typescript, n.d. [post 1954]; biographical
note on BB by his daughter, Dorothy Austin,
typescript, n.d.; 'Sir Basil Blackwell and
Merton College Library', annotated copy of
article, n.d.; cassette of programme on Radio
Oxford, re BB, 1987; correspondence,
photographs, etc., of briefcase 'dedicated' to
BB, 1983; 'Some Salient Dates in the Life of
Sir Basil Blackwell and the Growth of
Blackwell's', n.d.; photocopy of *Bookseller*, 4
March 1988, containing letter to editor re BB.

Honours and Awards
Papers re BB's honours and awards, incl.
Diplome de Grand Prix, Bruxelles, 1935;
Knighthood, 1956; Honorary Freedom of the
City of Oxford, 1970; Freedom of the
Stationers' Company of London, 1972;
Honorary Doctorate, Oxford University, 1979.

J. GUGGENHEIM   56 HIGH ST. OXFORD

*Nancy Blackwell,
mother of Benjamin
Henry, determined to
restore the family
name.*

Celebrations
Papers re BB's 25th, 50th and 70th
anniversaries of joining the company, incl.
photographs, press cuttings, guest list;
papers re BB's 70th, 80th, and 90th-94th
birthdays, incl. invitations, guest lists, menus,
letters and telegrams of congratulation, news
cuttings, photographs, texts of speeches.

Photographs
Black and white photographs, Merton College
Eights Crew, 1912, and Eights Week, 1913.
Photographs of Basil Blackwell, c.1925-1984.

In Memoriam
Obituaries; order of funeral service, St
Laurence, Appleton; lists of people attending
service and who sent wreaths; order of
memorial service at the University Church of
St Mary the Virgin, Oxford; text of
thanksgiving address by Henry Schollick at
memorial service; notice for buffet lunch at

Rhodes House; cassette of memorial service; correspondence re Henry Schollick's address at memorial service: list of recipients, letters of thanks, 1984.

Copy of *Report to Libraries* published by Blackwell North America Inc., 6 June 1984, containing obituary of BB; letters and telegrams of condolence on the death of BB, 1984; *Grace Before Going*, printed tribute to Basil Blackwell, 1984; black and white photograph of the opening of the Basil Blackwell Library at ASLIB headquarters, London, 1985; order of service for the dedication of window in memory of Sir Basil and Lady Blackwell, St Laurence's church, Appleton, 1994.

Christine Blackwell – 'our lady of the daffodils'

Miscellaneous

Joke book and loose examples of typos, amusing letters, letters from 'cranks', c.1937-72; *Sparks From An Old Flint*, vol. of manuscript poems inscribed to BB from William King (the author), Christmas 1930; menu for dinner at Stationers' Hall for Sir Stanley Unwin's 80th birthday, 1964; printed tributes to Sir Stanley Unwin, 1954, 1964; reviews of Sir Stanley Unwin's autobiography, by BB, 1960; letters of condolence to 'Toby' [Julian] Blackwell from Merlin Unwin on death of Sir Basil Blackwell, 1984; dinner menu for valedictory dinner for Sir Arthur Norrington at Trinity College attended by BB, 1970; article by Roger Cole on BB from the *Journal of the Oxford Society*, Vol. XXI., 2 December 1979; calligraphic manuscript poem, *Litterae Litterate – To Gaffer*, 1981; Christmas cards sent to BB, 1979, 1982; pen caricature on note paper, addressed 1 Linton Road, Oxford, inscribed, "For Mother", presumably by BB, n.d.; papers re Magdalen College School, incl. correspondence, 1965-82, annual accounts, 1963, school magazine, 1968, and quincentenary souvenir programme, 1980

Other Members of the Blackwell Family

Christine Blackwell

Degree certificate from University of London of Marion Christine Soans, 1st Class Honours in Classics, 15 December 1909

Dorothy and Sumner Austin

B/w postcard from D[orothy Blackwell?] to "Mrs Blackwell, Linton Rd", 1915; copy of *Oxford Journal Illustrated*, 21 November 1925, incl. review and photograph of *The Demon Hunter* in which Sumner Austin performed ; article by Sumner Austin in *Lilliput*, September 1950; copy of entry for Sumner Austin in *Who's Who*, 1980; obituary and order of memorial service, Sumner Austin, 1981; tribute by Henry Schollick at funeral service of Dorothy Austin, 1979.

Richard Blackwell

Obituaries, appreciations, orders of service for funeral, Tubney, and memorial service, University Church of St Mary the Virgin, Oxford, 1980; printed *In Memoriam*, 1984; papers re dedication of memorial stained glass windows at Tubney; printed leaflet about the Richard Blackwell Scholarship Trust, n.d.

Miles Blackwell

Order of wedding service and photographs, 1984; personal correspondence, 1987-94; correspondence relating to the award of an honorary doctorate of letters by Laurentian University, Canada, and letters of congratulations ,1990; copy of address given by Miles Blackwell on receipt of honorary degree at Southampton Institute, 1995; humorous cards, news cuttings, "funnies", collected by Miles Blackwell, c.1982-9

Philip Blackwell

Order of wedding service, Philip and Christine Blackwell , 1988

Elizabeth Blackwell

Eliza Blackwell: A Tribute and a Portrait, printed "In Memoriam", 1996

Blackwell Family, General

Conveyance between William Blackwell of Nuneaton and Thomas Wood of Leicester of tenement and cottage in Hinckley, Leicestershire, 1681 [this William Blackwell has no known link with the Blackwell family of Oxford]; carbon copy of letter from BB to John Owen of the *Oxford Mail* re Isaac Blackwell, 3 December 1975; copy of *Vogue* magazine, containing article on Blackwell family, October 1982; file of papers annotated 'no proven or direct connection', including correspondence with putative related families, family trees, etc., n.d.; a printed history of a Blackwell family in America, 1887-1937; correspondence between BB, and later Corinna Wiltshire, and John D. Blackwell of Canada relating to Blackwell family history, including copies of *Blackwell Newsletter* [Blackwell family history journal], 1979-85

Sarah Taylor: Maternal grandmother of Basil Blackwell (Lilla's mother)

SIR BASIL BLACKWELL'S DONATIONS TO THE MERTON COLLEGE LIBRARY

S IR BASIL BLACKWELL is among those who are remembered regularly during special commemoration services in Merton College Chapel. Along with such figures as Walter de Merton, King Henry III, Sir Thomas Bodley and other notable men and women, Blackwell's name is read out in the prayer in which the college community formally expresses gratitude to benefactors. Not least of Basil Blackwell's benefactions was the gift over a period of some thirty-three years of 28 early printed books to the College Library.

Basil Blackwell's first donation was the imposing set of six volumes comprising the Works of Aristotle in Greek printed in Venice by Aldus Manutius between 1495 and 1498. In the first volume is a hand-lettered label reading:

> Collegio Mertonensi erga adolescentem erga
> senescentem pariter benigno semper almo d.d.
> Basilius Blackwell alumnus non immemor MCMLI

> *To the College of Merton,*
> *equally kind to the young man and to the old man*
> *and always gracious, Basil Blackwell, who has not forgotten, gave this as a*
> *gift in 1951*

No doubt Blackwell, who read Classics as a postmaster (scholar) at Merton, composed this elegant and expressive dedication himself.

The Aristotle alone would have been a significant contribution to any library, but in Basil Blackwell's case it proved to be only the beginning. Dr Roger Highfield has

Detail from designs for Edward Bawden's Oxford showing the Radcliffe Camera crowned by an anatomical figure alluding to Dr John Radcliffe (1650-1714), royal physician and donor of the funds for the building.

told the story of how in 1955, as newly appointed Fellow Librarian, and following the instructions laid down in the seventeenth century that the college librarian should encourage gifts 'of bibliographical interest', he approached Blackwell about the possibility of another gift to the Library.[21] The unexpected result was a series of annual gifts of books, always chosen with care, that strengthened ties of friendship between donor and librarian (both scholars appreciative of fine books).

Fifteen of the books donated by Blackwell to Merton were printed by Aldus Manutius or his successors. This was not by chance. Manutius (*c.*1451?-1515) was a scholar who took up printing in mid-career. Working in Venice, he made every effort to produce texts of Greek and Latin classics of the highest standard possible at the time. He also believed that such books should be well made and aesthetically pleasing. The description could apply to Blackwell's publishing endeavors as well, and it is easy to see why he would enjoy selecting works of this particular printer for Merton. The Aldines donated by Blackwell include examples of ground-breaking large-format scholarly editions such as the 1495-1498 Aristotle and the 1513 Plato, as well as representatives of the smaller format octavos. The octavo format—a size that fits comfortably in the hand and is easily portable—was adopted by Manutius for a series of classic texts printed without commentary. Printed in the italic typeface designed especially for Manutius, these small books have been admired by scholars and book-lovers ever since they first appeared.

Several of the other books presented by Blackwell have Merton associations. There is, for instance, the *Microcosmography* of John Earle (elected Fellow of Merton in 1619). Another example is the fascinating *Manner of Making of Coffee, Tea and Chocolate,* dedicated to Sir Thomas Clayton, Warden of Merton from 1661-1693. The gift of these Mertonian books and of the Aldines exemplified the close connection between Blackwell and his Alma Mater, a connection now crowned by the gift of the Blackwell Collection.

The following list provides only brief details of the volumes given to the Merton Library by Sir Basil Blackwell. Fuller descriptions may be found in the Oxford University online union catalogue.

1. Apollonius Rhodius. *Argonautica.*
   Florence: [Laurentius Francisci de Alopa],
   1496. 4º.
   Presented 1955.

2. Aristophanes. *Works.* Venice: Aldus
   Manutius, 1498. Folio.
   First edition in Greek.
   Presented 1979.

3. Aristotle. *Works.* Venice: Aldus
   Manutius, 1495-1498. 5 vols. in 6. Folio.
   Presented 1951.

4. Aulus Gellius. *Noctes micantissimas* =
   Noctes Atticae. Venice: Iohannes
   Tacuinus, 1509. Folio.
   Presented 1970.

5. Boethius. *Works.* Basel: Heinrich Petri,
   1570. Folio.
   Presented 1981.

6. Catullus; Tibullus; Propertius. *Works.*
   Venice: Aldus Manutius, 1502. 8º.
   Presented 1966.

7. Cicero. *De officiis* [and other
   philosophical works]. Venice: Paulus
   Manutius, son of Aldus, 1541. 8º.
   Presented 1969.

8. Dante Alighieri. *Le terze rime = Divina
   commedia.* Venice: Aldus Manutius,
   1502. 8º.
   Presented 1982.

9. Dufour, Philippe Sylvestre. *The manner
   of making of coffee, tea, and chocolate.
   As it is used in most parts of Europe,*

*Asia, Africa, and America. With their
virtues.* Transl. by John Chamberlayne.
London: Printed for William Crook, 1685.
Presented 1969.

10. Duns Scotus. *In universam Aristotelis
    logicam exactissimae quaestiones.*
    Venice: Francesco Franceschi, 1586. 8º.
    Presented 1980.

11. Duns Scotus. *In primum et secundum
    Sententiarum quæstiones.* Antwerp:
    Joannes van Keerberghen, 1620. 2 vols.
    in 1. Folio.
    Presented 1964.

12. Earle, John. *Microcosmography: or, a
    piece of the world discover'd. In essays
    and characters.* London: E. Say, 1732.
    12º.
    Presented 1978.

13. Euripides. *Tragoediæ.* Venice: Aldus
    Manutius, 1503. 2 vols. 8º.
    First collected edition.
    Presented 1966.

14. Herodotus. *Historiae.* Venice: Aldus
    Manutius, 1502. Folio.
    Presented 1974.

15. Iamblichus. *De mysteriis.* Venice: Aldus
    Manutius, 1497. Folio.
    Presented 1968.

16. Martial. *Epigrammata.* Venice: Aldus
    Manutius, 1501. 8º
    Presented 1973.

17. Martial. *Epigrammata.* Edited by W.M.
Lindsay. Oxford: Clarendon Press [1902].
A.E. Housman's copy with his pencil
annotations throughout.
Presented 1958.

18. Overbury, Sir Thomas. *His Wife. With
additions of new characters, and many
other witty conceits never before
printed.*16th impression. London :
printed by Iohn Haviland, for A. Crooke...,
1638. 8°.
Presented 1982.

19. Ovid. *Works.* Venice: Aldus Manutius,
1502-1503. 3 vols. 8º.
Presented 1972.

20. Plato. *Works.* Venice: Aldus Manutius,
1513. 2 vols. in 1. Folio.
First edition in Greek.
Presented 1975.

21. Pliny, the Younger. *Epistularum libri IX.*
Milan: Filippo da Lavagna, 1478. 4º.
Rhodes, 1444.
Presented 1969.

22. Plutarch. *Vitae illustrium uirorum..*
Venice: In aedibus Aldi et Andreae Soceri
(Andreas Torresano), August 1519. Folio.
Presented 1971.

23. Richard of Bury. *Philobiblon.* Oxford:
Joseph Barnes, 1599. 4º.
With a dedicatory letter to Thomas
Bodley by the editor, Thomas James.
Presented 1960.

24. Seneca, *Works.* [Naples]: [Matthias
Moravus, for Blasio Romero], [1475].
2 parts in 1. Folio.
Presented 1962.

25. Seneca, *The workes of Lucius Annaeus
Seneca, both morrall and naturall.*
London: Printed by William Stansby,
1614. Folio.
Presented 1963.

26. Sophocles. *Tragaediae.* Venice: Aldus
Manutius, 1502. 8º.
Presented 1976.

27. Theocritus. *Idylls = Eclogae.* Venice:
Aldus Manutius, 1495 [1496]. Folio.
Presented 1980.

28. Xenophon. *Works.* Venice: In aedibus
Aldi et Andreae Soceri (Andreas
Torresano), 1525. Folio.
Presented 1977.

Basil (on the right) as an undergraduate, on the Merton barge

POSTSCRIPT

Tribute to Sir Basil Blackwell and fellow Blackwellians

The lines are fallen unto me in pleasant places: yea I have a goodly heritage.

SINCE MY FATHER'S DEATH, in 1984, I had been thinking of how to provide him with a fitting memorial. It was only when I retired as Blackwell's Chairman that my ideas began to take shape. Enlisting the help and sympathy of Rita Ricketts, I set up the Blackwell History and Archive Project. Little did I guess that in the course of the next three years 'my dream world', of what constituted 'a fitting memorial', would be realised. First, my father's lifelong commitment to the family firm was marked by restoring his old office in Broad Street, and setting up a standing exhibition of selected items from his archive. Although my father worked in this room from the day his father (Benjamin Henry Blackwell) died in 1924, the association is much longer. He started his life above this room in 1889 and played here as a child until his father commandeered it as a workroom, lining the walls with books bearing the B H Blackwell imprint. Secondly, some of my father's numerous writings and stories were published (R. Ricketts, *Adventurers All,* Blackwell's 2002) and woven into the social, political, economic and literary context within which my father grew up and the firm prospered. Thirdly, my father's old College, Merton, miraculously agreed to house the Blackwell Archive, thus preserving the firm's history. Fourthly, the Warden and Fellows of Merton agreed to name a room in Fellows' Quad: the Sir Basil Blackwell Room, to be opened at the end of 2004. My cup was full; I had not dared to hope that my father should find his way back to his much-loved College in such a way.

When I set out to meet the Warden of Merton, I felt much as my father had when he first crossed Merton's threshold: acutely aware of the privilege, although in most other ways my first serious acquaintance was very different from his. Among the papers now lodged at Merton are many accounts of my father's life in College. Writing of his trepidation and his insecurity on arrival, he describes himself as 'some twelve months younger than most of my year; a handicap I found difficult to surmount mentally and physically'. As his first term progressed, strong and close friendships began to develop, and by his final year he reported a distinct improvement brought about by a 'mind and body beginning to set'. Life at Merton in the early twentieth century was not made for the hedonistic, and resembled in essence the disciplined lifestyle my grandfather had followed as he attempted to improve himself. Merton provided a rigorous daily diet: Chapel before breakfast, a light lunch (Commons) after physical exercise on the river, or on the field (Rugger), and Evensong at 10pm every day. In those days my father was awoken at seven to the music of his 'scout' clearing out the fire grate, where 'by some sleight of hand, he kept (a fire) burning all day long'. My father would watch, rather guiltily, the 'nimble and cheerful Charlie Scarrott who combined in some measure the functions of valet, butler and chamber-maid, and worked seven days a week without the benefit of a summer holiday'. At the end of each day Charlie would cycle home with 'a bag on the carrier of his bicycle in which, like his fellows, he carried home to his family the broken meats from the staircase'.

My father later rejoiced when the old 'servant days' went, just as he applauded the growing presence of women in the College. In his days 'female undergraduates were remote mysterious creatures and chaperones were de rigueur'. But he remembered one who had attended the same Classics lectures. He 'rejoiced in her elegance and grace and discovered her name from a scrutiny of her bicycle. Verily, Phoebe W. had her reward; she married her history tutor'.[22] Devoid of other distractions, my father set out 'to grapple with the philosophical side of Greats', with the result of 'a Third in Mods (*valde deflendum*) and a Second in Greats (fair enough)'.[23] Although he may not have done himself full justice in the Examination Halls (it was my mother who was the classics scholar with a First from London University), his performance as a student oarsman was something to write home about: 'My strength had come fully to me when I rowed for the Eight at Six after nine days training with a delightful, rolling, splashing crew of freshmen. My sixth and last year was crowned with a bump supper'. 'Nunc, nunc, insurgite remis'; he had liberally interpreted as his rallying call: 'get more life off your stretchers'. And off his stretcher meant rowing. Four lines from Virgil's *Aeneid* summed up his feelings towards this 'austere sport' where even the most experienced individual feels like a nervous wreck unless lifted by the crew's unity of spirit:

> *Considunt transtris, intentaque bracchia remis;*
> *Intenti exspectant signum, exsultantiaque haurit*
> *Corda pavor pulsans laudumque arrecta cupido.*
>
> ·
>
> *Hos successus alit; possunt, quia posse videntur* [24]

In this way Virgil guided my father back to his studies. Rowing, for him, 'brought you back to where you started', having achieved a goal and circumnavigated the rocks below the waterline. But for all his attempts at high-mindedness, my father was irrepressible. And who better to be on the receiving end of his high spirits than the patient, if idiosyncratic, tutors. One such tutor was Walter 'Billy' How, who taught ancient history. As he taught, Billy How would allow his right arm to rise and fall to the rhythm of his words, giving emphasis to his addiction by using alliteration: 'Thus Pericles found it impossible to pursue a policy of peaceful penetration' for 'The day for which he had been sharpening his sword found him dallying with it in his sheath'. Finding himself in Billy How's tutorials with his closest friend Austin Longland, my father suggested a tease. The two friends mischievously conspired to prepare their next weekly essays, for reading to him, 'in a rivalry of studious magniloquence'. Come the tutorial, Basil, first into the fray, won the comment, 'Ye-e-es! Rather a tinkling symbol'. Longland, with a glint of anticipated triumph, followed with an utterance that my father admitted 'paled my ineffectual fire' and closed 'with a resounding period' whereupon he 'modestly dropped his eyes'. After a suitable pause, and a great deal of sighing, Billy How declared, 'Well, that's bad'!

On that occasion, Billy How was accompanied by a fellow tutor, the gentle philosopher H.H. Joachim, late Wykeham Professor of Logic. Joachim was equally loath to castigate the duo. He could only offer, 'Thank you; very interesting; will you have a cigarette?' The self-restraint shown by his long-suffering tutors embarrassed my soft-hearted father, who covered his tracks by offering up an 'original theory of knowledge'. Joachim and Billy How did him the courtesy of listening. Joachim then fell back in his chair exclaiming, 'God bless my soul'! It was suggested to Basil, by Edward Burney, wittiest of his contemporaries, 'that this was the first time he (Joachim) had acknowledged the existence of either (God or soul) and, Basil added, 'I was credited with his conversion!'[25] Whatever his tutors' views of this insouciant youth, Basil wrote that, for his part, 'he had only pleasant and grateful memories of the men who taught me'. Of others who taught him, he chiefly remembered 'the kindly H.W. Garrod, who presently turned from Classics to the field of English Literature after, as I suspect, a collision with A.E. Housman over the editing of Manilius, and W.H. Fyfe, Principal of the Postmasters'. Basil wrote that relationships with tutors involved more than just teaching: 'talking, walking and playing' was how he described their intercourse in those 'last golden days'. Still a regular visitor to his old College in his eighties, Basil wrote: 'I seldom enter my beloved College without a pang, for the names of so many of my contemporaries are engraved on the memorial' to those killed in War.

Turning over the pages of his Merton photograph album, my father would reflect on his student days, 'which were the golden sunset of our civilisation as Europe was poised to lead humanity into the new era of scientific savagery'. One memorable photograph dated 1908, and now in the Merton Collection, shows my father on an Oxford University Cadets training camp with a small, crossed-legged figure sitting at his feet, a figure later known to history as Lawrence of Arabia!'[26] There are other stories, too, of my father's indiscretions at Merton, ones that show the unpredictability of a life where town and gown overlapped. His friend and fellow student Adrian Mott remembered a garden party where 'Basil nearly came unstuck' while talking to a very pretty American girl. 'Suddenly she discovered that he was the unsympathetic beak (magistrate) who had fined her twice for bicycling offences. Never have I seen a woman so angry: in that decorous company she told him off like a fish wife: Never have I seen the majesty of the law so flouted, or its representative so taken aback.'[27] But holding forth in the company of Merton's students and fellows, however risky at times, was undoubtedly one of my father's greatest pleasures and one of his greatest hobbies in ripe old age. Nothing was to impede his speedy progress to Merton, where he ate lunch on an almost daily basis, and cutting straight across from the shop gave him the added pleasure of flouting Oxford's one-way traffic system.

Now with the housing of the Blackwell family and business archives at Merton, the two-way 'traffic' between Merton and Blackwell's will be guaranteed to flow again. If I could summon my father from the Elysium fields this posthumous 'flouting' would give him eternal amusement, but it would be nothing compared with his delight at being 'back' in the College's ancient library. And I can think of no more fitting memorial to him. Through the medium of the Collection, his stories rest side-by-side with those of the founders of B H Blackwell's and all those other Blackwellians who served the cause of learning and scholarship. What is more, thanks to Merton's generosity, their tales are beautifully explained in this catalogue. With the approval and backing of the Warden, the Librarian Julia Walworth, Archivist Julian Reid and Development Officer Jo Osborne, Merton agreed to publish a guide to the Blackwell Collection. The writing of this Guide serves as a fine example of the cooperation between town and gown that my father and grandfather helped to foster during their lives, and I would like to thank Julian Reid, Julia Walworth and Rita Ricketts for all their dedication and hard work.

The publication of this catalogue in January 2004 also coincides with the 125th Anniversary of the opening of my grandfather's 'little shop' on Broad Street. When B H Blackwell's celebrated its centenary, in 1979, my father was ninety. He might also have claimed to have up-staged the old despots that guarded the Sheldonian; in his eighty-third year they had been removed from their pedestals for restoration. A mortal Knight, it seemed, had outlived the emperors! My father had spent his life in the company of these emperors, flanked by the great buildings of the Sheldonian and the Bodleian. The Bodleian Library especially was an institution with which my father and his fellow Blackwellians maintained a symbiotic relationship. But if as he gazed across the road my father had recalled the Psalmist's words: 'The lines are fallen unto me in pleasant places: yea I have a goodly heritage', it would have been to Merton that his thoughts would have flown.

Julian Blackwell, Osse Field, January 2004

FOOTNOTES

1 Basil Blackwell's notes on books and functions of bookshops, published as an article 30 September 1952.

2 Roger Highfield, 'Sir Basil Blackwell and Merton College Library', *Postmaster* (1996), pp. 48 – 51.

3 See for example the juxtapositions in the diaries of Will 'Rex' King, a Blackwellian poet and antiquarian bookseller.

4 His grave singles him out as the founder of the Oxford 'Band of Hope'. He is variously described, for example as a French polisher, living in Blackfriars Road. Possibly another brother, William, came with them: William became a saddler and harness maker, living at 122 High Street, see Trade Directory 1853.

5 *British and Foreign Temperance Intelligencer*, 6 July 1839, pp 260-1, gives a report on the teetotal activities of B.H. Blackwell, who is described as 'Librarian'. This does not allude to his future as the City of Oxford's Librarian, but to his being the 'Librarian' of the Teetotal Society.

6 6 July 1839, pp 260-1, written by B.H. Blackwell, who is described as 'Librarian'.

7 A fuller account of the life and work of Benjamin Harris Blackwell, including his work as Oxford City's Librarian, is given in Rita Ricketts, *Adventurers All* (Oxford: Blackwell's, 2002).

8 From an undated account of his life by his granddaughter, Dorothy Austin. Dorothy and Basil Blackwell's mother, Lilla, must have had a chance to listen to the memories of Anne Stirling Blackwell, before she died in 1887, and must have passed on these memories.

9 See the letter from the Acting Warden of Merton to Julian Blackwell 29 October 1984.

10 Interview Basil Blackwell with Ved Mehta, *Books and bookmen,* January 1972, p 15.

11 Newsletter of the English Association, No 15, May 1984.

12 Diary, 1877.

13 Ibid.

14 Lilla and Benjamin Henry Blackwell married on 26 August 1886, Parish Church of SS Philip and James.

15 Notes on work etc contained in a notebook dated 1868.

16 Sir Basil's notes refer in this way to his mother.

17 From the notes of Dorothy Blackwell.

18 Scraps of drafts, mostly in pencil, are in Basil Blackwell's papers.

19 Letter Basil Blackwell to Angela Melvin, undated but after the death of his wife.

20 Richard Blackwell, notes on his father, 18 August 1976 and in a letter to Sir Arthur Norrington, 13 September 1976.

21 Roger Highfield, 'Sir Basil Blackwell and Merton College Library' *Postmaster* (1996), p 48.

22 This account of his life at Merton was written by Sir Basil for the Merton *Postmaster* in 1971 and reprinted in the Blackwell *Broad Sheet* in 1984.

23 Sir Basil Blackwell to Sir Arthur Norrington, 3 December 1975.

24 Aeneid, v 136-138,231 – Basil Blackwell's notes, A Dog's Ramble.

25 Draft for *Postmaster* 1971.

26 Basil Blackwell's notes for a *Postmaster* article, not the final version.

27 Notes, Sir Adrian Mott, 5 October 1954.